*Change*Wave
Investing

Picking the *Next* Monster Stocks of the New Economy

ChangeWave
Investing

Picking the *Next*
Monster Stocks
of the
New Economy

Tobin Smith

**Bard
Press**

ISBN 1-885167-35-0 *hardcover*

Library of Congress Cataloging-in-Publication Data

Smith, Tobin, 1957–
    ChangeWave investing : picking the monster stocks of the new economy / Tobin Smith.
        p.   cm.
    Includes bibliographical references and index.
    ISBN 1-885167-35-0
    1. Speculation. 2. Investments. 3. Stocks. I. Title: ChangeWave investing. II. Title.
    HG6041 .S64 2000
    332.63'22—dc21   00-024146

The author may be contacted through:
> Phillips International, Inc.
> 7811 Montrose Road
> Potomac, MD 20854
> 301-340-7788 *phone* / 301-340-0679 *fax*
> *www.ChangeWave.com*

A BARD PRESS BOOK
Austin, Texas

Editing: Cliff Avery
Copyediting: Deborah Costenbader
Proofreading: Charlotte Keith, Vista McCroskey, Luke Torn
Index: Alana Cash
Text Design/Production: Hespenheide Design
Illustrations: Hespenheide Design
Jacket Design: George Clemes
Jacket Illustration: Christian Ellis

First printing: April 2000

CONTENTS IN BRIEF

Contents

PART III:

THE PLAYBOOK: SCOUTING AND BUYING YOUR WAVERIDER STOCKS

PART IV:

PROTECTING THE LEAD: OWNING YOUR WAVERIDER STOCKS

Two Big Ideas

ChangeWave Investing is about your prosperity in the New Economy and two big ideas. The first big idea is how to profit from a New Economy stock-picking model that has delivered to its practitioners 150 percent annual portfolio growth since 1996. This model has allowed its users to turn tens of thousands of investment dollars into hundreds of thousands within very short time periods (12 to 18 months).

The other idea is a truly revolutionary way that you can capitalize on the greatest growth stock opportunities in the New Economy before the vast majority of the investing public. It's called open source investing.

Together these two ideas have allowed many Change-Wave Investing practitioners to catch many of the monster stocks of the New Economy and ride them into fantastic new wealth for their families. We strongly believe this will continue to happen, and we hope after reading this book you'll want to participate with us!

The Original Blinding Flash of the Not-So-Obvious

Believe me—starting a new approach to investment research and investing was the last thing on my mind when I began this journey ten years ago.

I have always been torn between two intellectual loves: the hunt for emerging growth stocks and the hunt for new customers—commonly called marketing. I am also incurably curious. One day about ten years ago, I asked myself, "Isn't analyzing and creating marketing strategies—figuring out how to dominate or sell more than one's competitors—the key factor in a company's success?"

My answer? "Yes."

"Then, wouldn't figuring out which publicly traded companies had strategies that were most likely to dominate or outsell their competitors be a key factor in a company's stock appreciation?"

My answer? "Makes sense."

From that fuzzy moment, I began a lengthy love affair with the crazy notion (at the time, that is) that picking winning stocks had more to do with analyzing their marketing and business strategy than with their balance sheets. In retrospect, the fact that I was not a trained securities analyst turned out to be advantageous—since I had no preconceived ideas or dogmas to overcome, I could make up my rules from scratch.

For years, I researched investment managers and investment strategies. And I came to the conclusion that the weakest part of their stock-picking research was their grasp of the marketplaces in which their companies competed. In particular, I found their grasp of market positioning—how a company's product or service uniquely and exclusively meets the customers' needs and wants—weak. (But understandable; it's the difference between a finance and a marketing perspective.)

My newly discovered marketing-centric approach seemed like an exploitable investment edge—analyzing companies on their capability to beat their competitors rather than how they looked on a spreadsheet business model. Little did I know how valuable the approach would be when a new form of enterprise—the Internet—erupted.

Another Observation

The observation I made throughout my multifaceted career in investment services, investment banking, and later in publishing and direct marketing was far less radical. First, you must know that I am a prodigious reader and an even more prodigious clipper of articles related to fields of professional and personal interest. The sheer cumulative effect of reading hundreds of magazines, newsletters, and books every month for the past 20 years or so caught up to me one day as I was reading one of my favorite magazines.

Forbes had an article on a little company called Orthodontic Centers of America, which had just gone public in 1993. At the time, I was working in the professional services marketing field and had been trying to convince professionals that to grow their practices radically, they needed to create a radical competitive advantage over other companies in their marketplace. My pitch was going nowhere.

As I looked for an example to show these docs what I meant, the Orthodontic Centers of America (OCA) article fit perfectly. Here was a company that was completely changing the way orthodontia was being sold, practiced, and positioned. They used retail advertising to drive traffic to their storefront practices. They redesigned their floor space and staffing to allow the doctors to see up to six times as many patients as their traditional colleagues. And gosh, they even came up with a killer offer: instead of a parent paying a $3,600 fee, half down and half in 90 days, patients could get most orthodontia for nothing down and $80 a month for 30 months!

Well, I loved the concept so much (note: the orthodontists I was working with *hated* the example) that I bought the stock (it quintupled), and I began looking for other companies that were using radical changes in strategic business design and strategic marketing advantages to grow their businesses faster than competing alternatives.

As I started researching other companies to add to my radical "change-maker" portfolio, an indisputable pattern emerged: the greater and faster the rate of fundamental change occurring within an industry, the greater the companies leading that change appreciated in value, at the expense of the second-best competitors.

ChangeWave Investing

I did not know it at the time, but this was the beginning of the core strategic analysis concepts we now call ChangeQuakes, Killer Value Propositions, investable ChangeWaves, and the No-Brainer Disproportionate Reward Rule. These concepts are the heart of the ChangeWave Investing program you are about to learn.

Fast-forward to 1995. Upon accepting a position as vice president and group publisher for Investment Publications at Phillips International, one of the world's largest investment advisory publishers, I finally could combine my two passions— marketing and stock research. I worked with many leading portfolio managers and investment analysts and soaked up their approaches to investing. Also in 1995, I started publishing my "ChangeWave Portfolio" of stock recommendations for friends and colleagues based upon the recurring pattern and relationship between the magnitude of change that a company brought to its industry and its stock price. In the inaugural ChangeWave Investing e-letter on December 31, 1994, the first five companies that I advised for purchase were

- America Online
- Orthodontic Centers of America
- QUALCOMM
- Medicine Shoppe International (MSI)
- Chantal

Chantal went broke. Orthodontic Centers of America rose about 600 percent before giving back about half, where it stands today. Medicine Shoppes International was swallowed by a drug distributor for a 150 percent gain. As you know, the other two companies and their stocks have experienced spectacular success.

I was now a bull-market genius. Still, my early success was but a glimmer of what the future would hold for Change-Wave Investing, which, by my reckoning, really started the day Marc Andreeson invented the Internet browser for the World Wide Web.

The Pre-epiphany

Most viewed the emergence of the World Wide Web in 1994 as the equivalent of CB radio—a nice little niche for nerdy guys to try to meet women. For a variety of now blindingly obvious reasons, I did not share this view. I soon became the outspoken (to put it mildly) leader of a small band of people at Phillips who foresaw great things for the Internet.

Mostly I suppose to get me to shut up at management meetings, I was charged with "experimenting" with ways for us to use the Net to market our various investment advisory services. This new assignment added joyful hours to my day researching the Net, meeting the early pioneers of the Internet business, and adding new pieces to the ChangeWave Investing strategy. Living in Internet time and making up the rules as we went along might not be for everyone, but for me it was (and still is) a perfect match for my nonlinear approach to life.

As I became more and more a student of the emerging New Economy ideas, I watched the stocks of the companies I was doing business with explode in value. I wondered: If the ChangeWave theory that radical change within an industry was the genesis of radical changes in industry-leader stock valuations, what would a radical change *within the entire economy* cause? Would the same pattern hold true for economy-wide reconstruction?

I really never dreamed the answer would, of course, be yes.

The Beginning of the ChangeWave Alliance and Open Source Investing

By the beginning of 1999, things began to come together. ChangeWave Investing had grown into a collaborative e-letter to thousands of friends, family, and New Economy professional colleagues I'd met in my Internet trailblazing. Many readers had become active participants in the ChangeWave game— helping me to find and analyze the companies that were the biggest beneficiaries of the radical, revolutionary change occurring all around us.

Interestingly, we found that the more WaveWatchers (as I called actively involved ChangeWave investors) participated in the discovery and analysis process, the better our results. And because our approach was different than the status quo, we created our own language for our concepts and strategies.

What we do in ChangeWave investing is simply ratchet up our wealth-building prospects by specializing in industries and marketplaces growing at least 100 percent to 200 percent a year. These companies in these spaces are growing their earnings and sales 50 to 100 percent per year—five-to-ten times the rates of growth in Old Economy industries.

By the middle of the year, it was clear our hardy band of WaveWatchers was making more money than we ever thought possible. The ChangeWave Investing strategy was leading us to invest exclusively in New Economy companies and markets—with breathtaking results. Many WaveWatchers had grown six-figure portfolios in less than 18 months following the program. More than a few literally became millionaires.

I began managing a private investment fund, ChangeWave Capital Partners I, to keep testing and improving the strategy with real money. The strategy continued to pass the test with flying colors.

The Epiphany

In early 1999, my day-to-day research led me to discover a fascinating book from a visionary named Eric Raymond, entitled *The Cathedral and the Bazaar.* Eric made a beautiful case for the "open source" software movement embodied by Linus Torvalds and his Linux operating system. His basic message was simple yet profound: "People do their best work when they are passionately engaged in what they are doing."

I knew I had seen the future. It was "open source investment research." My own experience with our crew of Wave-Watchers convinced me that if the word "investor" is substituted for "developer," virtually all of the principles of open source software development apply to investment research, particularly in the context of a rapidly and radically changing global marketplace. Just as no single programmer can do as good a job as a diverse group of programmers all working on the same project, no one company or research staff can possibly keep up with the rate and magnitude of change occurring in the globally inter-networked world we live in today.

As our earlier experience indicated, what we needed to make open source investment research work was people who were qualified and competent "programmers"—that is, credentialed professionals distributed throughout the global New Economy industries. We needed a discrete application— an investment model with a singular goal following a single investment analysis methodology or "playbook" that we all used and improved. Without such a system, all we had was a virtual Tower of "Babble." We knew we could have such a system by publishing our investing model in a book and by establishing a web site to provide support for WaveRiders everywhere.

ChangeWave.com 2000

In the summer of 1999, Phillips International agreed to be my partner in launching the ChangeWave Investing open source vision worldwide. I began to work on the book and our Phillips team began to develop our web site. *ChangeWave.com* offers a variety of valuable ChangeWave Investing research decision support tools for free to any and all investors—including updates on our investment model's central "core investment analysis logic." By the time you read this, the *ChangeWave.com* community site will be out of beta-testing and open to the public. Red Hat, Inc. is adding value to the open source operating system known as Linux by packaging it into convenient CD-ROMs, adding customer service support, and serving as a central open source code portal. In the same way, *ChangeWave.com* is adding unique value to the ChangeWave Investing's model "source code" by sponsoring and managing the ChangeWave Alliance—our network of credentialed, profiled New Economy professionals who are also ChangeWave Investing practitioners. In addition, *ChangeWave.com* is packaging the results of the investment intelligence-gathering and peer-review analysis process into a consolidated "buy/sell/hold" advisory service. This is available for those investors who just want the end-results advice and don't qualify or care to participate in the open source process.

Isn't This Just Like Stock Message Boards?

No. My hat is off to the Motley Fool brothers and the pioneers at Silicon Investor for their first generation open source investing work. But these come-one-come-all "stock-picking as entertainment" web sites or stock message boards frequented by enthusiastic people with God-knows-what basis or professional credentials behind their "posts" have some flaws. I've found the characteristics of making true open source investment research work are

- *One single area* of investment focus;
- *One model and source code* of investment analysis logic constantly improved via one master "key holder" to the system and thousands of colleague contributors;
- *Qualified and credentialed professionals* spread throughout the investment world exchanging a little of their time and expertise each month to participate in investment research projects in return for both psychological and financial rewards; and
- *A central communication* and analysis infrastructure and "home" where the intelligence can be gathered,

analyzed, processed, and electronically distributed to the digital communication device of your choice.

Our Track Record

In the last 48 months, money invested in emerging growth companies identified and evaluated by the ChangeWave Investing process has grown more than 2,500 percent—that is, our original investment capital grew 25 times bigger in less than half a decade. This growth rate on a compounded basis exceeds 150 percent annually.

We grew our aggressive growth capital more than 511 percent in 1999 alone. More important, every year our results have been getting *better* as the power of our open source approach has continuously improved our stock-screening and investing logic (see our track record in the appendix).

Where We Go from Here

To harness the power of ChangeWave Investing, you'll need to take a quick visit to the New Economy so that you understand what it means to you and your monster stock picking. We'll take you there in the beginning of the book.

Then we'll make sure you are up to speed in basic aggressive growth investing strategy.

Next, we'll cover the basic philosophical and economic assumptions and rules that are coded into the ChangeWave Investing application.

Finally, we'll get into core behavioral assumptions and rules we've included in ChangeWave Investing to mimic the pattern of institutional investing behavior.

At that point, you will be ready to get into the ChangeWave approach to screening and buying aggressive growth stocks. You'll discover that buying these highly volatile stocks well is easier than owning them well.

Our Mission for ChangeWave Investing:
The Network Is the Guru

- Bring low-cost, high-performance investment research to the masses through the "power of many—focus of one" strength of open source investing by sidestepping the current closed source, aristocratic middlemen that dominate the investment research world.
- Help both ourselves and our colleagues in Change-Wave Investing achieve financial security for our families by sharing our brainpower to find the best growth investments in the first decade of the twenty-first century.
- Have lots of fun and meet great people along the way.

Welcome to ChangeWave Investing!

Tobin Smith
Bethesda, Maryland
February 2000

ABOUT THE AUTHOR

Few, if any, investment strategists possess the combination of talents, accomplishments, and real-life business experience as Tobin Smith, founder and CEO of ChangeWave.com, Inc., managing partner and chief investment officer of ChangeWave Capital Partners L.P. (a private investment hedge fund), and vice president for Phillips International. In conjunction with Phillips, one of the largest direct marketers of investment advisory services in the world, Tobin launched *ChangeWave.com*.

Since 1980, Tobin has delivered over 500 seminars and speeches on investing, marketing, and strategic business development. As a marketing executive for over ten years in the investment banking and financial services industries, he worked for Bank Atlantic Financial Corporation, Security First Group, and First Reliance Capital Markets, Inc.

In 1995, he became vice president and group publisher of Phillips Publishing. He is editor of *ChangeWave Investing* and the weekly *WaveWire* electronic newsletter. As vice president of Internet venture development, Tobin launched the company's Interactive Media Group. It has been in these various roles as publisher, editor, Internet developer, and chief investment officer that he has refined the investment strategies and approaches featured in *ChangeWave Investing*.

He and his wife Marjorie reside in Bethesda, Maryland.

ACKNOWLEDGMENTS

The ChangeWave mission is to enable people all over the world to live significantly more prosperous and passionate lives within the rapidly ascending New Economy. The publication of *ChangeWave Investing* signifies the prime-time launch of this vision to the general public. And as with most audacious plans, a lot of people participated and led to its inspiration. They include:

Patricia Smith, for teaching me that we take risks, not to escape life but to ensure that life does not escape us;

Alan Bernstein, for introducing me to radical thinking and asking me what I wanted to be when I grew up;

Bob King and Richard Stanton-Jones, for teaching me everything I know about marketing and making people better off in ways they desire and will pay for;

John Coyle, Tom Phillips, and the entire ChangeWave.com team, for believing in a rather profane and off-the-wall anarchist, enough to join the mission and stake our professional lives together;

George Gilder, for his vision and courage to lead the thinking as to the possibilites of one world transformed into the equivalent of one massive fiber-optic semiconductor;

Mike Saylor and MicroStrategy, Inc., for envisioning a world where distributed, real-time intelligence replaces ignorance and empowers people;

Eric Raymond, for teaching us all what the power of the open source movement could be;

Carol Susan Roth, for gaining a valuable publishing partner in Internet time;

The crew at Bard Press and most significantly Ray Bard, for believing in ChangeWave Investing and working so hard to turn a stream-of-consciousness mess into a real book;

Cindi Leach and Jeff Davidson, without whom ChangeWave Investing would still not be finished;

And to my life partner and biggest supporter Marjorie Sutherland Smith, for hanging in for what has turned out to be one helluva ride.

PART I

THE PLAYING FIELD: HOW THE NEW ECONOMY IS CHANGING THE RULES

CHAPTER 1

Monster Gains from
Monster Growth Stocks

Ever feel like everyone is getting rich? Everyone but you!

The covers of *Time* and *Newsweek* tell the story of hundreds of thousands who are getting rich. Getting rich faster than ever before by investing in the stocks of the New Economy.

This is a time of radical economic change. This "monsterish" change offers a great opportunity for "monster" growth stocks. Stocks that grow more than 1,000 percent in 12 to 24 months.

In the '90s, 259 stocks rose 1,000 percent or more—a lifetime of growth for most investors earned by one stock in ten years. But the Top 20 monster stocks *grew on average* more than 27,000 percent!

Better yet, because we're only seeing the dawn of the New Economy, the last decade was just a warm-up for the 2000–2010 decade ahead.

The rewards of a few monster stocks can be life-altering. With as little as $5,000 and moves of 91,000 percent by Dell, 68,000 percent by Cisco, 66,000 percent by AOL, and 21,000 percent by QUALCOMM, you would have become a millionaire *five to ten times over* in less than a decade! And just think, for most of the last decade, the greatest wealth-making engine in history—the Internet—was just a nerdy toy.

The Risk of Staying on the Sidelines

The most important reason to dedicate a part of your investment capital to monster growth stocks is the risk of *not* investing in this revolutionary age. With so many explosive markets and stocks, the mathematics is too compelling to dismiss.

When you aggressively invest in the world's fastest growing companies, the most money you can lose is 100 percent. Yet many companies profiting from the New Economy revolution are generating investment returns of 1,500 to 3,000 percent, sometimes in as little as 12 to 24 months. This means you could literally invest $1,000 in 10 companies, have 9 stocks go to $0, and still make 10 percent on your money, catching only one 1,000 percent winner.

So you tell me—the most you can lose is 100 percent, and there's a good possibility that you can catch a New Economy wave-riding stock and earn a return of 1,000 percent-plus. Is that a bet you'd want to take with at least *some* of your investment capital? Can you really afford *not* to be in this once-every-hundred-years game?

Is it too late to play? This question is a bit like asking a young Henry Ford in 1917, "Is it too late to invest in the automobile business?"

Aren't We All Lucky to Be Living Now!

The conversion of our industrial age, mass-production, geographically restricted, physical asset–based economy to an intangible, digitally inter-networked, brain-powered, asset-

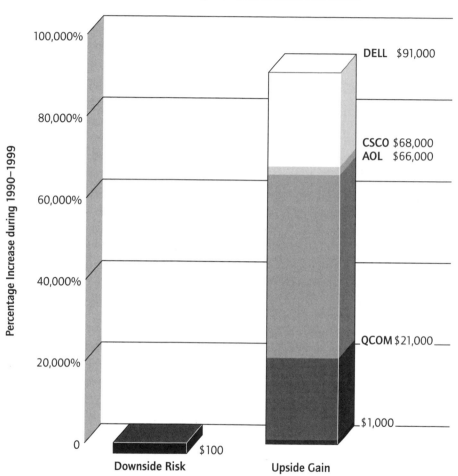

MONSTER GROWTH STOCK INVESTING

$100 Invested during the 1990s in These Four Stocks

based economy (what Alan Greenspan calls "idea-based value-added") represents a revolutionary change.

Even better for today's investors, inter-networked digital information technologies have emerged as a powerful, new economic lever for increased productivity. This has vaulted our economy into a period of hyper-change and hyper-growth at the same time.

We are indeed fortunate to be alive today and to have some money to invest. Why? Because, as with all the great economic shifts, this Third Industrial Revolution is likely to make as dramatic a transfer of wealth as the industrial age made with respect to its agricultural predecessor.

Becoming a ChangeWave Investor

ChangeWave Investing requires no Ph.D., MBA, or spiritual awakening. Yet, application of this strategy and stock-picking model has led us to recommend or purchase the stocks of companies that have appreciated an average of 150 percent a year since the dawn of the New Economy in 1995 (see the appendix for documentation). Compounded, that means about $50,000 in our growth and aggressive growth stock portfolios appreciated to more than $1.3 million by December 31, 1999.

Breathtaking results indeed. But what should matter to you is

- *why* those results occurred;
- why the odds of success weighed *less heavily* on us than other investment styles; and
- most important, why it's likely that when you practice ChangeWave Investing, the odds of success will continue to be on your side.

Is ChangeWave Investing for You?

It's likely that you can find a close description of yourself in one of the following four categories of investors:

1. **New Economy Professional:** You're right in the middle of the New Economy every day. You see the speed and impact of the changes going on. You now invest in companies that you believe have strong growth potential.

   For you, this book should be a quick read. You will understand the playing field and should quickly grasp the rules and the process outlined in the play-book. I guarantee your stock-picking and portfolio management performance will improve if you incorporate a good slug of our protocol into your investing. And you may even want to apply to join the ChangeWave Alliance.

2. **Traditional Investor:** You've been buying individual company stocks through a broker or by going online. You regularly spend time investigating companies and studying the market. You're ready to start building a high performance New Economy stock "sub-portfolio" within your existing holdings.

    You should enjoy reading about a new way to screen and invest. You may want to use the playbook alone or you may want to tap into the latest information provided by New Economy professionals at *ChangeWave.com.*

3. **Mutual Fund Investor:** Your strategy has been to let the "pros" (mutual fund managers) handle your investing on their own or through your 401k.

    If you're ready to take some of your money and make your own selections on the companies that will become the big winners in the next decade, the playbook will provide you step-by-step guidance. And, you can turn to *ChangeWave.com* to obtain additional helpful information.

4. **New Investor:** You haven't been a player but you see the huge possible rewards and want to get involved, yet you feel a little uncomfortable about playing on your own.

    You will need to read parts of the book more than once to learn the new language. The online information and guidance available at *Change-Wave.com* will be very helpful to you.

Are you ready to join the revolution?

CHAPTER 2

The Mother of All Economic Revolutions

Historically, the emergence of a new economic age has meant that more new wealth has been generated in the following 10 to 20 years than in the previous 100. We are currently experiencing the birth of a New Economy. What's particularly encouraging about your prospects for rapidly building new personal wealth over the next decade is that most of the experts in the New Economy believe this "mother of all economic revolutions" is only in the first inning.

Economic Productivity

Our institutions, the U.S. government, and most economists don't yet have a clue about how to measure the real impact of a globally wired, real-time world on our economic productivity.

A great example of this reality gap came October 28, 1999, when the federal Bureau of Economic Analysis decided to change the accounting rules on the purchase of software. The BEA has admittedly undercounted the value of software for years by treating it as a raw material to be used in the production of other goods and services. By changing the depreciable life of software from an immediate expense to a depreciable asset, expensed over its useful life, the BEA finally recognized that the useful life of software is longer than the minute it is first used. This one move recast the measurement of productivity for the past 20 years.

Now, I don't want to go off on a Dennis Miller rant here, but just wait until 20 years from now, when the "experts" abandon their 500-year-old accounting system designed to count bales of hay and widgets. They will go back and revise the productivity rates and reportable earnings of intellectual-asset or knowledge asset–based companies by 15 to 25 percent or more to the positive.

Harvard accounting professor Robert Kaplan says in the February 2000 issue of *CFO Magazine:* "Today, the long-term success of organizations comes from their knowledge-based assets—customer relationships; innovative products and services; operationally excellent processes; the skills, capabilities and motivation of their people; and their databases and information systems. Physical assets may be important, but they are unlikely to be as effective a competitive weapon as knowledge assets."

Highly respected Philadelphia Federal Reserve Bank economist Leonard Nakamura has pioneered the shift to this New Economy thinking. To paraphrase Mr. Nakamura, one day we will "learn" that what we really should have been doing all along is capitalizing the investments companies make in intangible assets instead of immediately expensing their development costs and deducting the expense from current earnings. On that day, everyone will recognize that intellectual property–based companies have for decades financially outperformed their Old

Economy, physical asset–based cousins by a mind-blowing order-of-magnitude difference.

Perhaps the famous management thinker and the original New Economy analyst Peter Drucker said it best in an interview with Kevin Kelly of *Wired* magazine: "Current economics is merely refining the obsolete . . . because economic theory is still based on the scarcity axiom, which does not apply to information. When I sell you a phone, I no longer have it. When I sell information to you, I have more information by the fact that you have it, and I know you have it. This property is not even true of money."

The Best Opportunity in 100 Years

To earn monster investment results, you have to live in a time of monster economic change. As noted MIT economist Lester Thurow points out in his book *Building Wealth*, you are lucky to be living in an age that will come to be known as the "Third Industrial Revolution." For the first time in history, the traditional sources of success—controlling physical and natural resources (land, gold, oil, and labor)—have changed. Physical assets are no longer the keys to building new wealth.

> Ralph Waldo Emerson told us years ago, "Not in his goals, but in his transitions man is great."

What's "new" about the New Economy is the key to building wealth today is substituting knowledge and information for physical assets. New wealth is being created by applying and leveraging rich information and creative brainpower through a radical new economic input—globally inter-networked, digital information technology.

Consider the great paradox of the Third Industrial Revolution, currently called the New Economy: Bill Gates, the king of this new digital knowledge economy, owns virtually no land, gold, or industrial processes. The book value (i.e., tangible financial and physical assets) of his Microsoft is $28 billion, yet the market value is near $500 billion.

Incredible Divergence

How does one explain this incredible divergence? More important, how does one account for the divergent valuation of thousands of other New Economy companies, driven primarily by ideas and brain-powered "knowledge capital," which enjoy market values 100 to 1,000 times their book or physical asset value?

The answer comes from a quick and painless economics lesson which Tom Petzinger, Jr. discusses in his New Economy article from the January 1, 2000, edition of the *Wall Street Journal*. In his insightful analysis, he asks us to think of an economy as the sum of every action people take to provide themselves and others more with less. In one way or another, wealth-creating innovations have *always* substituted knowledge or capital

Science fiction writer William Gibson once wrote, "You know, the future's already arrived. It's just not evenly distributed yet."

for energy, materials, or labor. The introduction of the three-field system (a form of crop rotation) in medieval Europe increased agricultural output as sharply as broadband datacom is contributing to communication today. In the nineteenth century, the steam engine replaced human and animal labor with mechanical energy. Ever since the invention of the wheel, this process has been the source of wealth creation and always will be.

In the New Economy, for the first time in history, more and more of the world's population is sharing its knowledge and information in real time via the Internet. Increasingly, this tool is facilitating and accelerating knowledge and information transfer, creating a whole new way for individuals and businesses to substitute knowledge and information "capital" for physical assets.

Capital for Labor

Because of this revolution we have another powerful traditional macroeconomic trend at play: the substitution of capital for labor. As Jeffrey Applegate, the profoundly accurate investment strategist from Lehman Brothers, pointed out recently, driven by the falling cost of technology, capital-goods prices are *declining* at a 4 percent annual rate, while labor costs are increasing at 3 percent. Says Applegate in the October 25, 1999, issue of *Business Week*, "If these [New Economy stocks] are not the growth stocks of our era, I don't know what are."

The ascendance of the New Economy has occurred as a result of the convergence of advances in microprocessors, optical communications technologies, and broadband datacom services. This is giving the world a new way for its people and companies *to provide themselves and others more with less by substituting real-time knowledge, information, and financial assets for physical assets and labor.*

More from Less

More economic productivity from less labor and physical resources. More for less. That's the big deal about the New Economy for investors. Because it is the companies with the greatest exposure to the future that are benefiting disproportionately in the financial markets and the marketplace alike.

It's indisputable: we've evolved from the industrial era to a knowledge era and a new form of wealth creation—knowledge capital. Alan Greenspan gets it; he noted recently that through the second half of the twentieth century, the U.S. tripled the real value of its output with no increase in the weight of the materials produced.

> What massive industrial disruption means to investors is simple—there are massive amounts of new wealth being made in front of your eyes. If you are looking to grow your wealth radically, you need to have radically changing marketplaces.

Nobody says the New Economy means that the laws of economics are repealed. Nobody says that the Old Economy is irrelevant. But it is clear that the physical asset–based world of commerce we politely call the Old Economy will consist of an ever-shrinking proportion of total economic activity.

WHEN DID THE OLD ECONOMY DIE?

- When Intel overtook General Motors and then General Electric as the world's most valued industrial company

- When Microsoft's market cap overtook the big three automakers in combined value

- When Microsoft's employee/market cap ratio hit $16 million per employee versus $154,000 per auto employee

- When Netscape introduced its user-friendly, downloadable browser in November 1994

- When the Telecom Deregulation Act was passed in 1996

- When in 1998, the 50 leading economists in the world missed their forecasts on U.S. economic growth by at least 50 percent for the fifth year in a row

- When corporate financial analysts opened their spreadsheet business models one day and lowered their inflation assumption for pricing, or

- When companies realized they had no more pricing power or ability to pass through higher labor costs to customers

Bottom line? To succeed in the monster growth stock game *this* decade, you have to come to terms with the reality that the New Economy is burying the Old Economy at a rate unseen since the last economy was buried in the late nineteenth century.

It is simply no contest.

A Tale of Two Economies

In their outstanding monthly *New Economy Watch*, New Economy experts John Browning and Spencer Reiss captured this idea very well in their response to a recent *Barron's* article which asked, "What can it mean when the market's most prominent sector boasts nirvana-like multiples, while much else trades at recession-level P/E's?"

According to Browning and Reiss, "It means that a new economy is being created, whose leading companies are remaking the landscape in ways that doom those who can't (or won't) change in order to keep up. The idea that there are two kinds of companies—those geared to the high-growth future and those clinging to the sinking past—should no longer be controversial, even to old *Barron's*. Today's markets are pricing companies on the assumption—correct, we believe—of a very different tomorrow. The point is that high growth—always a relative concept—is not coming back to the coal or steel industries any more than US Lead, one of the original Dow Jones Industrials, will dust itself off and rise from the grave. And it's worse than that: the old and infirm end up starved for investment while the young and strong swim it."

> Fortunes are won and lost in moments of transition, and the emergence of the third industrial revolution we call the New Economy is all about a moment of transition.

The rate of transition is staggering. According to *Business Week*, in the first half of 1999, New Economy manufacturing companies were boosting their output per worker 30 percent a year. At the same time, the Old Economy non-high-tech manufacturers were growing productivity by 2.5 percent. These New Economy companies boosted profits by 58 percent annualized rates versus the Old Economy's 8 percent. To put this in perspective, the New Economy industries accounted for approximately 19.6 percent of the U.S. economy in 1999 but earned 48 percent of the national corporate profit.

According to virtually all governmental and private forecasting outfits, by 2008, over 50 percent of the *entire* U.S. Gross Domestic Product, and 80 percent of corporate profits, will come from New Economy industries.

New Tech Beats Old Tech

I believe technology and information-based or leveraged companies are the chief beneficiaries of a permanently changed world. Most so-called value stocks are really old-tech companies in basic manufacturing, commodity production, and low-tech services. Old tech in the sense that

- Their products change slowly—cars, refrigerators, even air travel.

- They have no pricing power or ability to pass through higher labor costs.

- Consolidation through mergers or buyouts is the only opportunity to grow earnings significantly and then substitute capital for labor by investing in new productivity-enhancing technology.

Almost the complete opposite is true of new tech:

- New tech replaces old tech, and new tech replaces new tech, because new tech becomes obsolete every 12 to 36 months—generating more unit sales.

- New tech does not worry about cost passthrough because these companies learned long ago how to make higher and higher levels of profit via unit sales expansion while dropping the price of their products every year as a result of higher productivity.

- New tech volume grows because its products increase its customers' productivity—which in turn adds to volume growth.

Herein lies a formula for significant compound wealth building.

Acting as an Internet cheerleader of sorts, the Center for Research in Electronic Commerce at The University of Texas, Austin, has released a wildly optimistic Internet economy study sponsored by Cisco. The study predicts that if the Internet economy keeps expanding at its current pace, it will reach $1.2 trillion in revenues in three years, towering over the $1 trillion health-care sector.

After just five years, the Internet economy now rivals the airline ($355 billion) and telecom ($300 billion) industries in size, say the researchers. The study also reports that U.S.-based companies will generate more than $507 billion through the Internet economy in 1999, up 68 percent from the 1998 figure of $300 billion.

Internet-related jobs increased dramatically over the past year, going up 46 percent from 1.6 million to 2.3 million. Since revenue growth outstripped job increases between Q1 1998 and Q2 1999, revenue per Internet economy employee grew just 15 percent. The hottest Net sector by far is e-commerce, which has grown at almost double the rate of the other Internet economy segments:

Internet Economy Indicators

Segment	Q1 1998	Q2 1999	Growth
Infrastructure	$26.8B	$40.1B	+50%
Applications	13.9	22.5	+61
Intermediary	11.0	16.7	+52
E-commerce	16.5	37.5	+127

Source: *Center for Research in Electronic Commerce, The University of Texas, Austin, Oct. 1999.*

Final Thoughts

Today a rapidly growing body of American business leaders, investors, and knowledge workers are coming to embrace a new and disruptively powerful macroeconomic assumption: within this decade, intangible asset–based New Economy industries will grow in revenue and market capitalization to overtake and/or marginalize most Old Economy industries.

Current estimates by today's most accurate and relevant econometric analysts indicate that in the projected 15 trillion-dollar American economy of 2010, almost 75 percent of the market capitalization and GDP will reside within New Economy technology and knowledge-based service industries. Is it any wonder more and more investors find it riskier to own stocks in descending Old Economy companies than in the leaders of ascending New Economy industries?

The fact is, the time could not be better for you to get your share of this New Economy wealth explosion. Here's why. To paraphrase Gary Hamel, noted business professor at the Harvard Business School: in times of radical change, entrepeneurship become more important than stewardship. Said another way, in the early stages of any new economic system, the rewards go to those who create the new or attack the existing. And definitely *not* to those who preserve or defend the old.

Bottom line. If you believe the economic world today is comprised of three kinds of companies:

Defenders: Proctor and Gamble, IBM, Merrill Lynch, AT&T, Citibank, Barnes and Noble, Time Warner, The Baby Bells, the television networks, magazine publishers, et al.

Attackers: Amazon, Yahoo, AOL, E-Trade, Charles Schwab, Level 3 Communications, CNET, Covad, Z-Tel Communications, Netro Corporation, GM Hughes Electronics

Arms Merchants: Cisco, Sycamore Networks, Juniper Networks, Exodus, CheckPoint Systems, Clarent Corporation, VeriSign, Inktomi, Network Appliances, TIBCO Software

from which group do *you* think the odds are greatest that the next monster growth companies will emerge?

In short, the Attacking companies have the advantage in the New Economy against the Defenders. And the Arms Merchants are even better positioned—they sell their high-profit margin wares to both sides!

CHAPTER 3

Wall Street's Worst Nightmare— Open Source Investing

So, the New Economy is dramatically changing the world we live in. And new monster stock opportunities are popping up all the time.

Maybe you'd like an investment guru to help sort all this out?

Forget it.

There are no investment gurus in the New Economy—it's not possible. Even the visionary, proven New Economy geniuses like George Gilder, Kevin Kelly, and Alan Greenspan have mastered only a small piece of the New Economy puzzle. No one person can possibly get his or her arms around the radical change occurring these days. Common sense says that too much is happening too fast for any *one* person to make accurate, sustainable predictions about today's investment world.

There simply is no John Wayne in this economy to guide you. No hero that always knows what's right. It's up to you. And that's just as well, because most of the John Waynes of the

Old Economy had a way of riding into the sunset, leaving you in the dark.

So . . . if I'm not a guru or a John Wayne, then what qualifies me to write this book and expect you to spend time learning how to pick the next monster stocks?

I am a New Economy stock picker. ChangeWave Investing is my stock-picking model. This book details the model that's delivered 150 percent-plus annual gains since 1995. Good old all-American healthy skepticism could make you disregard ChangeWave Investing's past results. But we *are* on to something. Something bigger than gurus, something bigger than a magic strategy or system.

What we're on to is combining a proven New Economy stock-picking model with a new investment research "operating system" we have come to call "open source investing." Think of the ChangeWave Investing protocol as a software program or application.

The Open Source Investing Model

The term "open source" comes from the software industry. The term refers to opening up to everyone the "source code" that is the basis of any software program. Once he sees the source code, a programmer knows exactly how a software program works, i.e., he understands the logic behind the application (as opposed to "closed source" software like Microsoft Windows, which is proprietary and "locked").

The other part of open source software is that this source code is free—no one owns it and anyone who knows how to use it is free to do so.

The power of this collective, knowledge-based model is revolutionary. Once a programmer understands why a program works as it does, he or she understands how to improve it. And because, in the open source software world, this improvement is passed on to a central administrator and released to all users, the software is continually improved on

a real-time basis. Literally every day, it improves to the benefit of all.

The Power of Linux

The best example of this open source power in action is the
Linux computer operation system, originally created by Linus
Torvalds. Linux was born in response to the needs and desires
of web developers and web masters for an operating system
that was an order-of-magnitude more stable system than Windows NT (a closed source code operating system developed by
Microsoft) for their web servers.

Linux's developers' interest in this project was part personal and part altruistic: they were not getting what they
needed from Microsoft. And Microsoft's interests were dia-
metrically opposed to the interests of the group.

These renegade writers figured that by pooling their collective abilities, they could improve upon Torvalds' original
source code (which was posted on the Internet). Over time,
their ongoing work on the software reached the levels of
dependability they—and their spouses—desired (when Internet servers crash, it's the web master who gets the call at four
in the morning to fix it).

And don't forget the motivating factor of being able to tell
Microsoft to go to hell and take their crash-ridden code with
them.

Well, lo and behold, since the early '90s Linux has grown
to 8 million users worldwide and is the fastest growing server
operating system in the world. Another open source software
application, Apache, is now running on more than half of the
servers on the Net.

Hours and Hours

The big key to open source software's success? Development
hours. Quite simply, very few if any software companies, even

Microsoft, can muster the hundreds of thousands of development hours that an organized and motivated team of tens and hundreds of thousands of programmers can. It's no contest: the software with the most hours of development, testing, and debugging turns out to be the most reliable.

Another aspect of the open source movement is peer review: everybody sees what you are doing, and everybody is a qualified programmer. With thousands of *qualified* eyes (as opposed to chat rooms or unrestricted message boards visited by God-knows-who), *all* looking at the same piece of code, no wonder bugs in open source software programs get fixed so quickly and so well.

Blinding Flash of the Obvious

My blinding flash of the obvious? What if the open source approach was applied to investment research and analysis? The analogies between the two worlds were so strikingly similar, I was, for once in my life, speechless.

Open source investing is nothing but a widely distributed research platform. And when the open source development process is applied to a specific task like New Economy stock research, you get the same results you get in open source software—more reliable investment intelligence.

Why do I believe that the open source approach when applied to the ChangeWave Investing model has the same potential to achieve the incredible results that have been obtained in the software world? For starters, the track record of our initial foray into open source investing has been extraordinary. Measured in sheer profit performance, we have beaten (actually crushed) virtually all professionally managed indexes by margins of up to 20 to 1 for five years running.

But we don't think any one single investment approach is good enough to continue to outperform the markets. The game of aggressive growth stock investing moves too quickly.

To maintain your edge, you have to evolve at the same pace as the market—in fact, stay a few paces ahead. *ChangeWave.com* is the web site, modeled on Linux's open source principle, where a community of New Economy knowledge workers are dedicated to one goal: improving investing results by improving the ChangeWave Investing system's analysis, logic, and raw intelligence-gathering every day.

Nightmare on Wall Street

Who's the black-hatted villain who stands to lose a lot from our revolutionary method of open source investing? Here are a few clues:

- In January 2000, of all the stocks followed by more than 3,000 "sell side" securities analysts with 27,000 "buy" recommendations, how many "sell" recommendations were there? . . . 5,000? 1,500? Try 35. It wasn't always that way. In mid-1983, according to Zacks Investment Research, 26.8 percent of analyst recommendations were sells.
- In the decade of the '90s, how many "professional" managers of "growth" mutual fund portfolios beat the 500 stocks of the S&P 500? Half? A quarter of them? Try less than 9 percent; not even one in ten.
- Since analysts' claim to fame is their "inside" understanding of the companies they follow, logic would hold that they at least were pretty good at estimating earnings at the companies they so intimately follow, right? Not so. Most academic studies reveal that analysts' estimates of corporate earnings are wrong about 80 percent of the time.

Based on this dismal performance, you'd have to assume salaries for analysts and fund managers are *down* over the last ten years. Yet, salaries are *triple* what they were in the early '90s, and the average bonus for the top analysts in 1999 exceeded $10 million a year!

What the hell is going on? Call it Research Lite.

What securities analysts on the "sell side" of Wall Street (meaning they work for brokerage firms who sell stocks to investors) are selling today is not their ability to get inside an industry or a company to unearth the next monster stock opportunity. If they were, their salaries would be shrinking.

Clearly, they are paid for their ability to persuade investors to buy the stocks they follow. Or they're paid based on their ability to bring in tens of millions of dollars in investment banking fees from the same firms they are charged with "analyzing."

As long as money keeps pouring into mutual funds, managers will get their 1.5 to 2 percent, no matter how they perform. Them's the rules.

Now don't get me wrong—there are many fabulous securities analysts out there. And many are in the New Economy space. But what should matter to you is how will their research help *you* buy and sell the next monster New Economy stocks?

If the self-serving hypocrisy of Wall Street smells a little ripe to you, what are your alternatives? Is there a viable investment research alternative for individual investors who can't perform all the stock research they want and need for their portfolios?

There is. Just boot up the open source investing "operating system" and launch the ChangeWave investing model.

The Basic Logic

Consider this book the first draft of the basic model code—call it ChangeWave Investing 1.0. At *ChangeWave.com*, the source code or logic behind the model is open for all to see, understand, and improve. This book details the logic—all the assumptions and rules—that govern the ChangeWave Investing protocol. As in the software design world, in order to use the application, people will need to have a basic understanding of the logic behind the system.

It's important, too, that you learn the vocabulary of ChangeWave Investing, because it serves an important purpose. It puts us *all* on the same page, heading in the same direction and leverages the collective power of our brains, experiences, expertise, and networks. Concepts and terms are defined throughout, and the most important ones are included in a glossary in the back of the book.

In the context of open source investing, the ChangeWave Investing model simply describes proven aggressive growth stock discovery and analysis boiled down into a step-by-step, connect-the-dots application. The protocol you are about to learn mimics the strategies and behaviors of successful aggressive growth investors much smarter and much more experienced than I.

The beauty and strength of ChangeWave Investing is that every day, with the power of our open source investment network and the "focused curiosity" of New Economy professionals, valuable new intelligence and knowledge arrives into the ChangeWave system. Every day, this distributed thinking and downstream body of knowledge, logic, or intelligence is tested and validated, improved, refined, and redistributed to the community in real time . . . both by members of the ChangeWave community and by our team of investment analysts, researchers, and support staff.

INSTANT REPLAY: HIGHLIGHTS OF PART I

- The New Economy created by the Third Industrial Revolution offers an opportunity to participate in astounding growth and reap potential rewards far outweighing the risks of sitting on the sidelines.

- In the '90s, 259 stocks rose 1,000 percent or more. This should just be the warm-up for the 2000–2010 decade ahead.

- The New Economy is rapidly outpacing the Old Economy. In 1999, the New Economy made up about 20 percent of the U.S. economy but accounted for almost half the profit. By 2008, projections indicate that the New Economy will be 50 percent of the overall economy with 80 percent of profits.

- There are no all-knowing investment gurus in the New Economy.

- The network is the guru. Using an open source platform and a common discovery and analysis model, ChangeWave Investing draws on the power of inter-networked, credentialed New Economy professionals to find New Economy stocks poised for massive growth.

PART II

RULES OF THE NEW GAME: LEARNING ABOUT CHANGEWAVE INVESTING

CHAPTER 4

The Roots of a New Idea

To understand the hows and whys behind any investing model, you must look at its fundamental philosophical assumptions. Here's the ChangeWave Investing wisdom most relevant to the success of aggressive growth investors for the upcoming decade.

The Philosophy of Pragmatism

Much of the core of the ChangeWave Investing approach comes courtesy of William James, the great philosopher and father of the school of philosophy known as "pragmatism." Most investors are pragmatists: they want positive results from their investments.

James believed that one knows an idea is true if it is useful. In the context of aggressive growth investing, this means that the only valid proof of your stock selections is if other people come to the same conclusions as you and buy those stocks also.

James also believed strongly that knowledge could be rightly understood only in its context. In investing, this means that the current and future value of a company has to be considered in the context of what's really going on in the world in which the company exists and competes.

Appropriate Context

ChangeWave Investing puts your investment idea into the appropriate context of what is happening today. We start our hunt for the top 10 percent of New Economy industrial sectors we call SuperSectors (ranked by secular growth rate). Then we apply our stock-picking logic to determine the very best positioned subsectors or spaces from the top to the bottom of the value chain.

We do this top-down drill for one reason: the cascade effect of economy-wide growth emanating from mass economic shifts or changes in demand and buying behavior. This cascade, or "ratchet effect," is the old domino game applied to the economics of growth. This means that when an irreversible or what is known as "secular" change in demand occurs across all economic sectors, the smaller sectors of the economy, the ones that actually sell or do the stuff that enables this shift to happen, grow 10 to 20 times faster than the rate of the economy-wide change itself.

These broad-based, trillion-dollar secular economic transitions we call Monster ChangeWaves are like a mountain-wide avalanche rolling into a narrow canyon. When this happens, the relatively slow-moving mountain of snow turns into an explosive cannon spewing out the smaller end of the canyon.

To aggressive growth investors like me, this cascade effect is another way of saying that when you get the investing opportunity context right, or the really big growth picture, you greatly increase your odds of screening away everything but the fastest growing beneficiary spaces and stocks.

The main reason we built *ChangeWave.com* and sponsor the ChangeWave Alliance Network is to broaden the richness of context and the reach of observation beyond a single individual's capability. By "plugging into" the vast richness and reach of ChangeWave Alliance's credentialed and trained network, you can add literally hundreds of qualified research hours to the richness and reach of your personal knowledge and experience base.

In Times of Revolution, Invest in the Arms Merchants

I find it easier to impart this timeless philosophy via a simple parable.

"So, Grasshopper," the old man says, "you have come a long way to find out how to secure your fortune in this decade by riding the monster growth stocks of the New Economy revolution. How did you find me?"

Responds the boy, "How else, Master? Yahoo! I searched under 'most handsome and richest New Economy stock picker.'"

Says the old man, "You're smarter than you look, kid. Here, then, is the answer you seek: Fortunes are won and lost in moments of revolutionary transitions—it is true. But in revolutions, two men always get rich. One is the arms merchant—the one who sells the bullets and guns of battle to the warriors. The other is the man financing the arms merchants. When there is a war on, Grasshopper, don't invest in the warriors doing the fighting—buy the companies selling the bullets and the companies financing the arms merchants. No matter who wins the war, both sides must buy bullets and arms. You will get rich.

"But be careful to invest in the arms merchants supplying the battles for the highest stakes, for these are the battles for which the combatants will expend all their bullets and armies till death or victory. Remember, also, that no matter which companies win the battles, if you back the arms merchants serving the biggest, most ferocious battles, and their financiers, you get rich."

The lad inquires, "But master, which battles should I select? How will I know which battles will be the largest and most ferocious? How will I know which of these arms merchants to invest in?"

"Ah," the master smiles. "For this you must learn the ways of ChangeWave Investing. They have developed a very effective way of selecting the most ferocious battles and best arms merchants and financiers to invest in."

"But, Master, ChangeWave Investing? Are not you mixing your metaphors?"

"Yes, Grasshopper, but whose book is this anyway?"

"Can you teach me the ways of the ChangeWave investor?"

"Yes, I can. But only if you promise to use this wisdom wisely and share it with others who could benefit from a few extra million bucks in their retirement nest eggs by 2010."

CHAPTER 5

Twenty-first Century Value Investing

A big, radical part of the ChangeWave Investing philosophy is our perception as to what
value investing really means in the context of
the New Economy. Traditional value investing
is buying stocks of misunderstood physical
asset–based companies and waiting for the rest
of the world to come to understand their value.
This, ChangeWave Investing is not.

If you're seeking a more clever way to buy
misunderstood cyclical and Old Economy physical asset–based stocks at lower prices and sell
them at higher prices, ChangeWave Investing
ain't for you. Trying to outguess 7,000 analysts
driven by investment banking fees and fighting
it out every day to earn average market returns
in companies like Philip Morris, Alcoa, or International Paper is not the way to realize monster
stock gains.

But I do believe the practice of Change-
Wave Investing is a modern form of "value"
investing. Stay with me on this one. To my way
of thinking, our sweet spot is taking advantage

of the misunderstood nature of intangible asset–based and knowledge capital–based industries and companies. These are the companies that invest in and develop patented and copyrighted intellectual property, knowledge processing, and information and leverage them into high-priced, high-profit-margin proprietary products and services.

How Misunderstood a Company Is

Now, let's take the great value investor Sanford Bernstein's definition of his approach to value investing as described in his Spring 1999 client newsletter: "It's not how good a company is that counts most," says Sandy. "It's how misunderstood a company is that counts most. A company does not have to be outstanding for its stock to outperform; it needs to be better than people think it is."

My case? Virtually everyone breathing today agrees that valuing intangible assets is clearly the most misunderstood part of investing. So, isn't investing in the fastest growing, intangible asset–based companies before the investment world comes to a common understanding on how to value intangible assets just a modern form of traditional value investing?

Our Hybrid Form

In our hybrid form of value investing, we simply ratchet up our wealth-building odds by specializing in industries and market spaces projected to grow at least 100 percent a year in the foreseeable future. These companies in these spaces are growing their earnings and sales at least 10 to 20 times the rates of growth in the Old Economy industries where the "value stocks" live.

Dividends? Don't give us 45 percent-plus tax rate (state and federal) taxable dividends. We invest to reap the benefits of the Last Great American Tax Shelter left to private investors: the ability to sell a radically appreciated stock and pay a 20 percent capital gains tax on our profits.

And why don't we screen by traditional fundamentals like P/E's, EBITDA (earnings before income tax, depreciation, and amortization), and other Old Economy metrics? In the revolutionary economic world of explosive growth markets of the early twenty-first century, historic standards of analytical economic measurement, or "metrics," plain don't work.

Meet Bill Miller, the "value" mutual fund manager famous for being the only such manager in America to beat the S&P 500 Index every year of the '90s. Mr. Miller tells us, "Traditional metrics, when they work at all, work best with traditional businesses. The value of these traditional analytical tools is usually a function of the historical data supporting their effectiveness. It is true that some of the best technology companies have rarely looked attractive on traditional valuation methods, but that speaks more to the weakness of those methods than the fundamental risk-reward relationships of those businesses.

"For example, Microsoft has appreciated in value almost 1 percent a week for 14 years. Companies don't outperform year-in and year-out unless they were radically undervalued (or misunderstood) to begin with."

Proxy Valuation

Without a set of valuation rules to go by, growth investors have to come up with a set of measurements or metrics that they feel approximates current valuation reality. In investing, this is called a "proxy valuation" method. This approach allows us to take the massively misunderstood but very real value of a company's intangible assets and come up with an approximate value range. The ChangeWave Investing proxy places a company in context with the size and rate of growth of the fastest secular growth markets in the economy. Then it rates the odds of the company's becoming the dominant or co-dominant "owner" of its space.

In our proxy valuation formula, we figure that the company with the greatest odds of dominating one of the fastest secular growth spaces in the economy possesses, in our view, the most currently valuable intellectual property on earth.

Thus the ChangeWave Investing process is, in effect, a New Economy growth-stock valuation tool. It's a proxy method for identifying the stocks most likely to rise in value based on

- the power of their proprietary patented intellectual property;
- the size of the opportunity they are aimed at; and
- the strength of their strategic positioning to capitalize on the opportunity.

In reality, this basic formula has validated itself in almost every marketspace within the New Economy industries (read knowledge or information-based industries) for over the past 20 years. If the market speaks, you gotta listen . . .

Intangible Asset Paradox

Our bet is that this intangible asset paradox—i.e., the disconnect between how valuable intangible assets are versus how they are treated in financial statements—will eventually be solved.

To my thinking, admittedly in the minority, true "value" investing in the context of the New Economy means buying companies

- with the most misunderstood business assets— intangible assets,
- in the fastest growing parts of the economy,
- where their proprietary intellectual property and intangible assets can be leveraged and sold at very high and sustainable gross profit margins to create the most insurmountable competitive advantage and strategic lock-in.

Listen, when people argue that "the value of a stock is the net present value of its future earnings," I do not disagree. I do point out, however, that the other part of the textbook definition of stock valuation is that common stock is also a "call" or share on the assets of a company. That is, *all* the assets of a company—both physical and intangible.

Since the primary assets of a company are not recognized by traditional accounting, I argue that the only place they can be valued is in the security valuation mechanism we call the public stock market or in the private market.

My conclusion to the intangible-asset paradox?

That the value of a publicly traded stock today, by definition, has to reflect the net present value of the future earnings *as well as* what the market assesses the stockholder's call value is on both the physical and intangible assets of the company. Many are now calling this the "option" value of the company, which includes the value that leadership of a Super-Space can mean to a company (i.e., first call on new strategic alliances, first opportunity for merger candidates, etc.).

In short, until the government catches up with what clearly is a huge reality gap, you tell me a better way to establish the call value of the intangible assets of a company *other than* market-based asset pricing, in which people reach into their wallets to buy stocks in the public capital marketplace.

CHAPTER 6

ChangeWave Investing 101

Think of the ChangeWave Investing stock-picking model as a disciplined approach to the sport of aggressive growth-stock investing. Our goal in publishing our stock-picking model is to reduce much of the "art" of New Economy stock picking to a more repeatable science.

Sports Metaphor

Thus the game plan from here on is simple: we're going to use good ol' all-American sports metaphors to illustrate the art and science in the practice of ChangeWave Investing.

- Successful aggressive growth investing is "the game."
- You are the "scout" searching for great investment "prospects" (companies) to "draft" onto your "team" (your portfolio).
- The stocks are the "players" who represent their companies.

- The New Economy is "the playing field."
- The ChangeWave Investing model is your "playbook."
- The market is your "opponent," constantly trying to beat you by faking you out and making you guess wrong.

Seven Steps

There are seven steps in the ChangeWave Investing process:

Step 1. Decide to play: Your first decision is whether you're going to be a player or whether you're going to sit on the sidelines and watch others reap the gains in the monster stocks of the New Economy.

Step 2. Decide how much money you want to invest in New Economy stocks: Whether it's $100,000, $10,000, or a smaller amount, you need to decide what initial amount you feel comfortable with. The most important thing is that you get started.

Step 3. Decide where you want to invest and how much risk you want to take: Here you determine which "leagues" (which represent three SuperSectors with different risks) you want to invest in, what percentage of your money you want in each league, and how much you want to invest in each player (company). Chapters 13, 14, and 15 will provide you information for this step.

Step 4. Make a draft list of "talented prospects": Here you make your preliminary selections of the companies you have an interest in drafting (buying). Chapter 16 will assist you with your selections.

Step 5. Complete worksheets on your best prospects: Here's where you do your homework and determine which stock is the right stock in the best space. They're almost always the big winners. Chapter 17 will provide you information for this step.

Step 6. Buy your high conviction stocks: After you have completed the WaveRider draft worksheets you'll have the supportive information to buy your stock with high conviction. Chapter 18 will prepare you for this step.

Step 7. Own your stocks well: Here's where the discipline comes in. You will need to hang tough during the down markets, sell your poor performers quickly and unmercifully, and add to your strongest positions. Chapters 19 and 20 will help you.

ChangeWave Screening Process

The ChangeWave Investing strategic screening process is a discovery and analysis protocol that sequentially builds an airtight rationale for buying stocks. Practicing the ChangeWave process over the past four years has allowed me to detect and invest in the most highly investable moments of disruptive change within industries and companies months before most of the rest of the investing world is able to see them and place their bets.

Why does the process work so well? I believe it's because we have "deconstructed" the prevailing core logic and philosophy of aggressive growth investing into a sharper, more focused approach. We're able to cherry-pick the best-of-the-best sectors and companies out of the larger, less profitable universe that most investors are considering. Said another way, it's the markets and stocks we choose to ignore that make a difference.

SCREENING STOCKS
The ChangeWave Investing Process

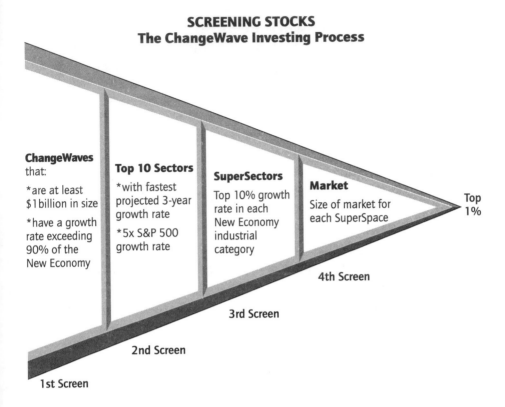

ChangeWaves
that:

*are at least
$1 billion in size

*have a growth
rate exceeding
90% of the
New Economy

Top 10 Sectors

*with fastest
projected 3-year
growth rate

*5x S&P 500
growth rate

SuperSectors

Top 10% growth
rate in each
New Economy
industrial
category

Market

Size of market for
each SuperSpace

Top
1%

4th Screen

3rd Screen

2nd Screen

1st Screen

The ChangeWave Investing stock-picking process helps you to make accurate decisions through these four key screens. Our goal is to help you screen all the publicly traded stocks down to the top 1 percent or so before you decide which one to buy. How's that for putting the odds on your side?

CHAPTER 7

What Makes Stocks Go Up and Down?

What makes stocks go up and down? More investment capital flowing into a stock than is flowing out of it. In other words, more buyers than sellers.

In free-market capitalism, growth investment capital moves for essentially three reasons:

- It moves toward the most predictable secular growth opportunity.
- It moves away from the reverse— predictable slowing growth.
- Last but not least, investment capital moves because someone believable is doing a good job of selling a stock's growth story. On Wall Street that's called "sponsorship." You must never forget that stocks are, in reality, no different than any other product or service: they need to be merchandised and sold or they sit on the shelf without selling until they are drastically discounted.

You may find it helpful to think of the stock market like this: it's simply a daily worldwide voting machine. Every day, people vote with their investment capital on how optimistic or pessimistic they feel toward the prospects of a company's rate of sustainable future profitable growth. These "voters" more often than not come to their conclusions based on how easy it is to understand and believe the logic behind a stock's growth story and how believable those are who are telling the growth stories.

The Movers and Shakers

You undoubtedly have heard of the popular concept of adoption curves or product life cycles. It's where the term "early adopter" comes from. The concept is that you can group people into subsets based on where they tend to land on the so-called "adoption curve" for new products or services. Years of testing conclude that your position on this adoption curve is mostly hard-wired into your personality. It is this hard-wiring that makes the behavior repeatable and measurable.

From earliest to latest adopters, these groups are called

The Innovators: These people are the earliest to welcome and adapt to new things—the bleeding edge. About 3 to 5 percent of the world.

The Early Adopters: This group represents the next 10 to 15 percent of adopters. Not bleeding edge, but leading edge.

The Early Majority: These are the early pragmatists who say "I need solid evidence (and peer pressure from the early adopters) before I act." About 34 percent of the world.

The Late Majority: This is the "I need conclusive evidence to buy" crowd (who also need peer pressure from the early adopters). Another 34 percent.

The Laggards/Nonadopters: Enough said.

How does this relate to stock buying and selling? Here's a news flash: People buy stocks the same way they buy other products. The same predictable behavior that causes people to buy new products carries over to stocks.

The basic strategic logic applied by most professional growth investors is simple handicapping—making an educated guess as to the future perceptions of other investors. As the famous economist and incredibly successful investor Lord Keynes said when asked about his secret: "If you're going to bet on who's going to win a beauty contest, don't bet on who *you* think is most beautiful, but who you believe the judges think is most beautiful."

Three Types of Players

Three types of players play the aggressive stock investing game. The *fundamental players* try to figure out which stocks the judges (i.e., other investors) will think most beautiful via good old-fashioned fundamental research and analysis. These strategists are innovator and early adopter investors; they make their money being early and right. With direct and indirect analysis, they form their "investment thesis" or Big Idea as to why they think a particular stock or sector of stocks will become beautiful (or more beautiful) in the eyes of the marketplace. They usually buy stocks long (i.e., betting they will go up in value) and tend to hold their positions the longest.

In the next camp are the *technical traders,* who use technical analysis (bar charts and graphs of stock price movements and trading volume patterns) to decide which stocks are poised to move up or down more than others. This camp includes mostly early majority investors. Many technicians do look to fundamentals after they have spotted a stock that is exhibiting patterns they like. But they believe first in the recurring behavioral power of human nature and the recurring nature of specific stock movement patterns; it is their main criteria for forming their blinding flashes of the not-so-obvious.

Then there are the *momentum investors*. They are late majority stock adopters. Beauty to them means positive, increasing price and earnings momentum—stocks with a trend line of higher earnings and higher prices. They usually subscribe to a form of Newtonian physics which holds that "a beautiful stock is one that is in an upward motion because they tend to stay in that upward motion—until they don't." When the upward movement stops, or the positive earnings growth slows, momentum investors sell immediately.

Aggressive Growth Stock Valuations

Most institutional fundamental-based investment managers, as part of their stock-picking debate evidence, try to figure out what a stock is going to be worth a year or two after they buy it. These future stock valuations come down roughly to the same formula: the future price of the stock is equal to the future earnings of the company times the future price-earnings ratio (i.e., the multiple people will pay in the future for what they perceive to be the company's future earnings). The higher the price-earnings ratio, the higher the value.

For growth stocks, three factors combine to determine the future P/E:

- The rate of earnings growth.
- The perceived consistency of earnings growth.
- The "excitement" factor.

The excitement factor can best be applied to a company with an apparent sustainable competitive advantage that can be parlayed into domination of a vast, rapidly expanding secular growth industry.

When Wall Street can make an argument that a company has the competitive goods to become the dominant company in a long-term, rapid-growth industry, it gets excited. The simplest and most compelling logic of this argument comes when a company is growing its market share more than 15 percent per year and/or is growing its profit margin faster than its competitors and faster than most other industries.

The only kind of company that can deliver this kind of performance is one with a locked-in advantage over its competitors. It has to have something the marketplace wants and needs that other providers cannot easily replicate or deliver. Thus, in Wall Street's eyes, evaluation of sustainable competitive advantage is the main event in judging the beauty contest. So evaluating a company's competitive advantage and its sustainability, ahead of Wall Street, is a crucial puzzle to solve.

Competitive Advantage

Back to Economics 101 for a second. Competitive advantage in a free and open marketplace is ultimately derived from providing better value for equivalent cost to a market of customers (better known as a "strategic differentiation control point" to marketers) or equivalent customer value for a meaningful lower cost ("a low-cost provider strategic control point").

Securities analysts look to the strategic control points, because in a fast-growing marketplace, the greater a company's strategic control over its customers, the greater the predictability of its earnings growth. The most valuable strategic control points a company can possess, New Economy or not, are built-in barriers for their customers to switch to other companies and that command virtually insurmountable barriers to entry from competitive alternatives.

In the agrarian economy, land and resources determined who won and who lost. Michael Porter, the eminent Harvard business strategy professor, teaches that controlling the value chain in the industrial economy is the basis of competition. And, the company that most controls that value chain wins.

In today's New Economy, where knowledge, information, and the replacement of labor for capital are emerging as the currencies of competition, strategic control points are becoming intangible things such as databases, brands, copyrights, two-year development leadership, and even unique organizational design or hard-to-replicate business model design.

To securities analysts, these things can be quite beautiful. And since the value of companies from now on will increasingly be enhanced by their intangible assets, we judge the value of a company as a strategic aggregation of intangible assets and how they are used to create a competitive advantage within the world's fastest growing new marketplaces.

A Five-Minute Course in
Investable Change

For me, the study of economics would have been a lot more interesting if it were repackaged and entitled "How to Make $1 Million a Year Investing in Radical Change." Particularly if I had known that, in 1999, I would actually make millions of dollars applying what I'd learned from that course in the real stock market.

Aggressive investing is not a democracy. Money flows to the highest areas of sustainable (i.e., noncyclical) growth, called "secular growth" areas, and seeks the most likely beneficiaries. Just like in life, where everyone is not a top 10 percent or "A" student, not every area of our economy qualifies as a top 10 percent secular growth industry. In the last few years, technology stocks have been attracting a disproportionate share of investment capital because people believe they will have the highest growth potential.

Investable Change

Knowing the difference between a killer investable opportunity—"investable change"—and a noninvestable event is the first key to successful aggressive growth investing.

Let me start with a definition: *Investable change,* or what we call a ChangeWave, is at minimum a $1 billion economic transition or transformation within an industry, economic sector, or entire economy whose sustainable growth rate exceeds 90 percent of the other growth areas in the total economy.

Notice I use the threshold of 90 percent. What most people miss when they get excited about the growth prospects of their favorite stock is "relative to what?" You may be onto an interesting growth story, but it needs to be interesting compared to all the other stocks that can be bought.

ChangeWave Investing focuses on generating and marshaling investable intelligence to discover *investable economic transitions* that direct us to the highest secular growth areas of our economy. We call these growth areas SuperSectors and their subsectors "SuperSpaces." The most likely beneficiaries of investable change we call "WaveRider" stocks.

Incremental Change

We ignore incremental or "noninvestable" change. Here's why. Incremental change is synonymous with linear change—change that improves the status quo. Suppose you build a Ford Fairlane. Then you add tail fins. You still have a Ford Fairlane—now it has fancy tail fins. Years go by, and you add air bags. Now it is a safer Ford Fairlane. No matter how many modifications or improvements you make, it is, in essence, still a Ford Fairlane. Souped up, jazzed up, but a Ford Fairlane.

Another way to characterize investable change is in the term "discontinuous change." What would represent discontinuous change? As outlined in the tech-investing classic *The Gorilla Game*, discontinuous change starts a "discontinuous innovation." An example: Miracle Motor Co. invents an electric car that rides on air and has force fields which make it impervious to crashes. Give people a car that can't crash, doesn't need gas, and will drive anywhere, and you change the *concept of driving*

Management theorist Peter Drucker said that for a product or service to be adopted readily by consumers, it needs to be perceived as having *ten times* the value of its predecessor.

forever (not to mention the concept of a family vacation).

So, you ask, why don't air bags represent discontinuous change? Don't they make the car much safer? The air bags inflate automatically. The consumer doesn't have to think or even do anything and—whoosh. This is not discontinuous change because the innovation did not obliterate the old way of driving.

Would everybody rush out and get the floating, impregnable electric car? No. Some people love their old car and wouldn't trade it in no matter what came down the pike. Cost would deter some people. Safety is much more important for some than for others. In time, however, the car with force fields would gain widespread acclaim. Magazines would tout its features. All car manufacturers would begin to adopt the standard. Soon, it would be difficult to find a dealership that was not offering the new vehicle.

Discontinuous innovation is the front door to an investable event. Incremental change is a trap door.

Strategic Inflection Point

In his classic book *Only the Paranoid Survive*, Andy Grove, chairman of Intel, uses the mathematical term "strategic inflection point" to mean the moment in time when the old strategic picture of an industry dissolves and gives way to a new means of doing business: "A strategic inflection point is when the balance of forces shifts from the old structure, from the old ways of doing business, to the new . . . It is a point where the change curve has subtly but profoundly changed, never to change back to the old again."

My term for a strategic inflection point is a "ChangeWave." Mostly because I flunked statistics, I assume it's easier for non-math people to understand the concept of a wave of change, rather than an inflection point.

ChangeWaves, the Beginning of New Wealth

To find rapid wealth-building opportunities, you have to find the rapid, significant secular changes we call ChangeWaves.

Secular change can be triggered by mass commercialization and adoption of new technological, regulatory, or strategic capabilities or innovations. Entrepreneurial companies harness these innovations and create new, order-of-magnitude (i.e., ten times) improved ways of doing things people already do. Or better, they invent new ways of doing things people always wanted to do but couldn't, until the new capability was harnessed and incorporated into an old process or product.

James Watt's steam engine cut the cost of mechanical work by 90 percent and kicked off the first Industrial Revolution. And the invention of circuitry-etched silicon annihilated the cost of computation and gave rise to Intel, Microsoft, Sun, and Cisco.

Visualize a quiet pool of water. If you drop a small pebble in the pool, it creates small ripples or waves. If you drop a huge boulder in the pool, it creates much larger ripples or waves. Large secular change, such as the steam engine or the microchip, is like the large boulder creating ChangeWaves throughout the economy.

When there is a nonlinear (or out-of-the-blue) order-of-magnitude thing that makes people change or quit doing the old thing, you have the beginnings of a market shift or transition. Once a critical mass of people discover the tremendous value of doing something in a new, order-of-magnitude-better way, they never go back to the old way. They are converted. This is what I mean by transformational change.

As part of this process, old companies who cannot adjust quickly enough to the new, order-of-magnitude-better way of doing things go out of business. As the great economist Joseph Schumpeter said, "Capitalism is a process of creative destruction . . . By nature, capitalism is a form or method of economic change that not only never is, but never can be, stationary."

A Good Thing

Ironically, for the aggressive growth investor, the fact that the majority of people—investors, managers, and institutions—still don't get our completely reframed economic picture is a good thing. In fact, a large part of our success in ChangeWave Investing depends on human nature and the FUD (fear, uncertainty, and denial) that accompanies an economic transition of this magnitude. Thanks to this, variable rates of recognition and response to radical change are as hard-wired into our individual personalities as are our levels of smell and touch.

There is a law for this phenomenon: the Law of Disruption. First identified by the very insightful team of New Economy consultants, Larry Downes and Chunka Mui, the law postulates that where "social systems [read people] improve incrementally, technology improves exponentially." In other words, there will always be a gap between the early graspers of the new and the pragmatists waiting for "clear evidence" before they accept that change has actually occurred.

The Law of Disruption also means we can have an edge in our personal wealth-building during times of great disruption. Because as aggravating as the grim reality of Old Economy thinking and behavior is for those of us who work with these head-in-the-sand Luddites, there is a marvelous silver lining. For without the head start the pragmatic, late-adopters to the New Economy continue to give us, our investment results would not be nearly as dramatic.

Blinding Flash of the Not-So-Obvious

When our ChangeWave Investing research prepares us to pick a stock, we call this highly profitable moment of "pre-common knowledge" a "blinding flash of the not-so-obvious." But this is not enough to select stocks successfully. To gauge the potential of a company and the space in which it competes, you have to put the space and company in context with all the others.

This is where 99 percent of all investors fail. ChangeWave Investing puts industries and companies into context with other opportunities you have to choose from. By boiling down the New Economy industries into the Top 10 SuperSectors and the Top 20 SuperSpaces (which are constantly updated on *ChangeWave.com* and available to you free of charge), you can view your own blinding flashes of the not-so-obvious in the context of other investment spaces and stock opportunities with the click of a mouse.

ChangeWaves Made Simple

As you now see, a ChangeWave is simply a best-of-class, highly investable, no-brainer secular growth trend assumption or thesis. What makes ChangeWaves so highly investable is that when lots of growth investors start making the same no-brainer growth assumptions about certain parts of the economy, there's a bunch of money to be made owning the companies that Wall Street believes will be the primary beneficiaries from the trend.

CHAPTER 9

Three No-Brainer Rules That Govern Stock Appreciation

There are rules that determine human behavior and the movement of investment capital. These are like universal laws that govern the way people and institutions act. Here are three rules that are powerful forces in determining your ability to create wealth by investing in the market.

The No-Brainer Predictability Rule

We know investment capital moves toward the most obvious sustainable growth, and it moves away from the most obvious risk of slowing growth. The key word here is "obvious."

> *The right stock in the best space gets the money.*

But what comprises the best sector and the best space? Most aggressive growth investors with capital to invest seek an answer to the following basic questions before they place their bets:

- "Where is the fastest, biggest, and most locked-in sustainable growth in the economy today?"
- "Which sectors are biggest beneficiaries of this huge, predictable, and sustainable growth?"
- "Which companies are best positioned to capture a disproportionate percentage of this locked-in growth?"

When institutional investors come to what they feel are the most obvious, "no-brainer" answers to these questions, they move their capital *out* of areas that are most predictably at risk of slowing or low growth, and move it *into* the areas of the highest or most obvious predictable rates of sustainable growth. It is the "obviousness factor" or degree of confidence in future growth predictability that makes capital move toward or away from a sector or a stock. A torrent of money gets aimed at this "strategically advantaged" or positioned space when a majority of aggressive growth investors come to the same no-brainer conclusion or what we call a "group blinding flash of the obvious."

We, too, follow the simple logic that the bigger the predictable secular growth opportunity, the larger the amount of cash that will flow toward it. And the greater the flow of capital into a sector, the higher the most strategically advantaged stocks within that sector or space will rise in value.

The No-Brainer Disproportionate Reward Rule

To understand why seemingly rational institutional growth investors are fixated on finding and owning the dominant company in potentially huge markets—and why they will pay astronomical premium prices once they feel they have found them, go back to how you played marbles. Remember?

Winner takes all.

Aggressive growth managers believe in "leaders-take-most and winners-take-all," because in nine out of ten cases, the industry winner does take all. As in *all* the profits, *all* the industry valuation, and *eventually*, virtually all the business.

The most predictable winner in a top secular growth space goes to the highest market valuation—every time.

Rajiv Chaudhri, the very successful portfolio manager of the Digital Century Fund, speaks well for the groupthink behind this most firmly held rule of almost all aggressive growth investors. And, although he invests in information technology companies primarily, the law and perspective he speaks about apply as well in any brain-powered information industry.

As Chaudhri explains in *Barron's*, May 10, 1999: "It is very important to identify the future winners of any potential large market . . . As markets become larger, the number of really successful companies becomes fewer and fewer, and at the end of the day, there are one or two companies at the most that really dominate and walk away with the bulk of the industries' profits . . . and valuation. We've seen this in microprocessors (Intel). We've seen that in PC operating systems (Microsoft). And in dozens of smaller industries, too."

Game-Over Dominators

These are the most predictably profitable stocks to own. Here's our definition of "game-over dominators":

- the number one and number two contestants in a commonly acknowledged rapid secular growth industry—"Emerging Game-Over Dominator" ("E.G.O.D."), or
- the number one player who happens to dominate one subsector within one of the most commonly acknowledged rapid secular growth sectors—"Game-Over Dominator" ("G.O.D.").

When investment managers find two or three companies competing as emerging game-over dominators in a soon-to-be-discovered industry, I call this the leaders-take-most play. They buy the emerging dominators with more than 15 percent market share and let them fight it out.

Once a stock becomes commonly recognized as the number one or number two emerging game-over dominator in an acknowledged high secular growth industry, both stocks will soar until one stock is crowned the game-over dominator (G.O.D.) stock. In an industry perceived to have years of rapid growth ahead, that stock's value is virtually certain to grow to a valuation that exceeds all the other competitors in the industry combined.

For example, in the high-growth storage-area networking software space, Veritas and Legato had been vying for dominance. It was a seesaw battle, but in late 1999 Veritas pulled ahead, and then Legato reported very disappointing earnings.

Boom—Legato crumbles and Veritas goes on to gain another 50 points. To institutional investors, Veritas is now the odds-on game-over dominator of this 200 percent a year growth space, and it has a market capitalization value larger than all other now marginalized competitors combined.

This behavior is as predictable as the coming of spring and summer.

According to Chaudhri, "When the dust settles in any information technology-based industry, there will be one company with 60 to 70 percent of the market share and the bulk of profits and valuation in that segment. The number two guy will have a 20 percent share." And the rest . . . who cares?

But why is this winner-takes-all rule so predictable?

The Human Element

Let's get anthropological. Anything in life that is highly predictable and involves human beings is due to innate human nature. Individually, one can achieve changes in personality and behavior. En masse, however, human beings are quite predictable. Evolution is an ongoing, extremely slow process. As a species, we may exhibit greater awareness, increased sensitivity to certain issues, and even flashes of evolving into a more rational and balanced type of creature. But for now, it's a safe bet that human nature will follow some fairly predictable courses.

Each of us is hard-wired to make decisions that we believe will enhance our position, outlook, or longevity. We instinctively seek to make the best of situations in our own self-interest throughout the day, week, month, year, and throughout our careers.

Commerce originated because individuals sought to fulfill human needs. People make choices based on the value propositions that commercial vendors offer. A person's decision to buy from one company versus another and to buy one product or service rather than another boils down to a simple equation:

$$\text{Value} = \text{Perceived Differentiation} \times \text{Emotional Payoff's Relevance to Me}$$

This equation is a fancy way of saying that every individual is going to judge what is most valuable to him or her based on self-generated criteria. When it comes to technology, what's highly predictable about this age-old maxim is that individuals will still choose what is most valuable to them, not necessarily the best technology.

Case 1: Tale of the Tape

Betamax and VHS videotapes were introduced around the same time. From a technical standpoint—as anyone in the television and film industry will concur—Betamax is clearly superior. It offers sharper picture, higher resolution, and a host of other advantages. Yet, VHS became the standard.

Why would anyone choose VHS over BETA? Because the purveyors of VHS had stronger marketing and stronger distribution, generating more favorable articles in the press, and did a better selling job to national retailers, among many other reasons. So VHS became the standard.

Soon, anyone who wanted to tape the NBA finals or a favorite movie or create home movies quickly realized that most recorders and camcorders used VHS and most retailers stocked only VHS. What's more, friends and relatives were using VHS cassettes. It became in an individual's own best interest to purchase VHS cassettes.

Case 2: The Dirty on QWERTY

The same phenomenon occurred with keyboards. The QWERTY keyboard is inferior to the Dvorak keyboard. The QWERTY was devised more than a hundred years ago to *slow down* typists. If the QWERTY designer had put the most commonly used letters in the middle of the keyboard, the keys carrying the letters to the platen would jam. By putting the "a" and the "e" in distant locations and the "n" and the "t" and the "s" away from each other, fingers strike the keys slightly slower, thus allowing clunky, manual typewriters to perform adequately.

As technology improved and later as the entire society adopted PCs, the rationale for QWERTY keyboards disappeared. In the digital age, it flat out makes little sense. Keyboard manufacturers worldwide know this, yet consumers, and institutional and retail buyers, including PC distributors, have stuck with QWERTY keyboards.

Why? They are the keyboards most people learned to type on and so they are the ones they want to buy. The decision to purchase technology is never entirely based on who has the superior technology, but rather on who has the technology that the purchasers want. People tend to demand comfortable, low-risk products.

Managers of large investment portfolios understand this tendency and base many of their investment decisions on it.

The stocks they purchase for their constituents typically represent companies whose products and services offer the least risk and highest predictable growth.

Industry Standard

Investment managers understandably gravitate toward companies who have the de facto standard in an industry and a one-stop-shopping solution for customers (a "closed loop"). In every industry you can name, companies are trying to establish the de facto standard. This is also known as the natural advantage, technopoly, or monopoly. The winners emerge as game-over dominators, and their competitors are the wannabes.

Cisco, for example, sells 80 percent of all telecommunication routers and dominates its niche because it hit a critical mass and became a predictable closed-loop solution in its industry. Cisco satisfies many emotional wants and needs of both its customers and its institutional investors. If I'm an institutional investor, and I buy Cisco stock, I can take a weekend off. If I have a bunch of Cisco-like stocks, I can take a few weeks off. If I can lock in the stock of a game-over dominator and rest easier, I'm going to do it. In fact, I'd buy three times as much of their stock, rather than divert that money to one or two other companies whose stock might make it, but who would make me nervous.

The No-Brainer Disproportionate Reward Rule applies to any commercial endeavor. Why are familiar brands so successful today? First, the human brain can handle only so many stimuli at a time. If I see two boxes of corn flakes on the supermarket shelf and one of them says "Kellogg's," I have a good idea of what I'm going to get for my money. If the other box of corn flakes is the store brand, however nutritious, well-packaged, and competitively priced it is, my inclination is still to buy the brand-name product. While studies show that in many cases store brands exceed the value of brand-name products, they never sell as well.

In a world of rapid change, brands become the touchstone of familiarity and reliability, justified or not. Low risk, reasonable comfort—let's buy some more. This is why stocks in dominant companies and industries are valued at five to ten times higher than the lesser players. Think of our game-over dominators as the "leading brand."

Predictability

Predictability is a powerful attractor, as the following example attests. Say you have children. You move into a new neighborhood, and you are looking for a high school for your freshman son. School A has a track record of graduating 89 percent of its students to college and 14 percent to the Ivy League schools you promised your Dad, on his deathbed, that his grandson would get into. School B is brand new with fabulous facilities, a renowned staff handpicked from the finest schools. It boasts the finest computer system in the country. But it has never graduated anyone to anywhere.

Which do you choose—School A or B?

At first blush, the fancy new school may be attractive. But I bet if you add the emotional baggage of the promise you made to dear old Dad, you'd feel a lot better opting for the school with a proven track record.

The very same emotional issue is faced by aggressive growth portfolio managers every day. When there are time-tested strategies for picking winning stocks that have proved themselves over and over again, why load up your portfolio with dubious stocks? Who wants all the anxiety, all the uncertainty, when you can go with the predictable formula?

The No-Brainer Logic Rule

Stock selection at most investment firms is a unique form of debate, and whoever delivers the strongest argument for or against the purchase or sale of a stock usually wins—i.e., that stock gets picked for the portfolio. This leads us to yet another ChangeWave Investing rule, the No-Brainer Logic Rule:

> *All things being equal, the simplest to understand secular growth and competitive advantage logic wins the growth stock debate.*

Take the November 1999 UPS stock offering. How could they raise $6 billion in one day for a business that has not changed in 50 years? Think about the case for buying the stock. As opposed to having to understand TCP/IP technology and the difference between COBRA and Java Bean architectures (remember: 90 percent of growth money managers know little more about technology than the buzzwords), you could make the case for UPS in a terse phrase: *50 percent dominant delivery agent for e-commerce companies growing at 200 percent a year.*

The company with the easiest to understand sound-bite, secular growth, and competitive advantage logic wins the stock-picking debate.

The Sound-Bite Corollary

There is a related rule or corollary to the No-Brainer Logic Rule.

> *Nobody has the time or the intellectual bandwidth to consider any Big Idea or thesis for more than a couple of minutes.*

Now this might come as a shock to some of you, but most aggressive growth investment managers have the attention span of the average three-year-old. I have watched this phenomenon for years, and after managing money myself, I know why this pattern is so prevalent.

With dozens of new stocks coming into a money manager's universe every month, and literally a thousand different variables to juggle every waking moment, the human reaction is to reduce the most current thinking on the great investment puzzles to manageable sound bites.

Because money managers think this way, a company has to reduce the components of its Big Idea to the easiest to understand and believe sound bites.

Since no stock gets going or keeps going without big money behind it, the logic behind your Big Investment Idea has to be easy for the big money players to come to understand and accept—a no-brainer.

What our investment mantra "the right stock in the best space" and the no-brainer rules mean to you is that, when armed with a massive no-brainer secular growth assumption, Wall Street will come to same conclusion as to which stocks they should buy to payoff their "insight."

This is why it is so important to become a good handicapper of Wall Street's *next* no-brainer secular growth assumption or ChangeWaves.

CHAPTER 10

The Ripple Effect of ChangeQuakes

Like dropping a boulder in a pool or the movement from an earthquake's epicenter, there is a natural effect from the rapid changes happening in the New Economy. These ripples or waves create a cascading value chain of relationships that begin with initial change and go all the way down to individual companies. Earthquake-like changes occur often in the New Economy, creating disruption, new products, and services—and new investment opportunities.

The ChangeWave Investing process systematically examines these ongoing waves to determine their impact on industries and companies. This screening process increasingly focuses on the companies that will be the beneficiaries of these cascading changes. And, in doing so, provides information about which stocks have the greatest growth potential.

Starting at the top of the chain, we examine each of these major points where change has a major impact. When you understand this chain

THE VALUE CHAIN

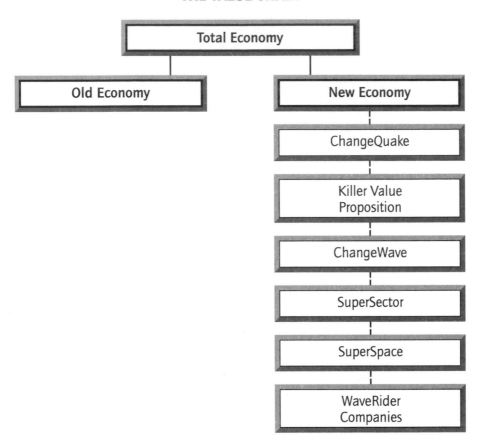

of events and understand the ChangeWave Investing process, you can dissect any industry or company and determine its likelihood of becoming a great investment opportunity.

ChangeQuakes

A *ChangeQuake* is an eruption of new, potentially transformational technological, regulatory, economic, or strategic capabilities within an economy. ChangeQuakes create new environments in which companies can provide new Killer Value Propositions (KVPs), which can be turned into investable opportunities. These Killer Value Propositions send Change-Waves emanating into the marketplace. There are four kinds of ChangeQuakes.

Technological ChangeQuakes come from technological break-throughs. An example is the adoption of a worldwide standard for high-speed data transfer over copper telecommunication lines. This makes possible an order-of-magnitude difference in transmission speed between a 56K modem and a 5MB Digital Subscriber Line (DSL). DSL service is simply a Killer Value Proposition created or packaged from a ChangeQuake.

The technology behind DSL was first created by a company named Aware, Inc. and called ADSL. When DSL is offered to consumers and the order-of-magnitude improvement in online speed is valued, a ChangeWave forms from the old way to the new way.

In late 1999, a new technological standard, called "Blue-tooth," for sharing data between any computing or wireless device was adopted. When an entrepreneurial company develops a way to package this technology in a way lots of people won't want to live without, we'll have ourselves a Killer Value Proposition. A ChangeWave from non-Bluetooth-enabled devices to Bluetooth-enabled devices will form.

If the Bluetooth-enabling sector meets our minimum growth criteria, chances are we'll have ourselves a new Super-Sector and a few pure-play Bluetooth WaveRider stocks to buy.

Regulatory ChangeQuakes change the rules within an industry and bring a new capability into the marketplace. For instance, when the SEC changed the rules of the brokerage industry from fixed commissions to open-priced commissions, we had a discontinuous change or ChangeQuake. When Charles Schwab packaged the capability into a new service called "discount brokerage," it created the Killer Value Proposition (90 percent lower commissions) that attracted millions of investors away from their conventional brokers. That launched the ChangeWave called "the discount broker revolution."

Strategic ChangeQuakes occur usually within an organization when a new business model or process creates a powerful new capability. A company can then package this new model or process into an order-of-magnitude-improved Killer Value Proposition. In recent years, Dell Computer's direct selling business model is the best example. The key to a strategic ChangeQuake is determining if the new capability is difficult or nearly impossible for industry competitors to copy. If the new capability is not virtually copy-proof, it's not a discontinuously changing capability. It's just another feature that everyone will soon emulate.

Strategic ChangeQuakes can also occur as order-of-magnitude shifts in strategic direction for companies with unique or proprietary capabilities. In this case, the ChangeQuake is usually a new CEO like Lou Gerstner at IBM or Michael Eisner at Disney. If a new CEO massively changes the strategic plan of the company to significantly enhance the power of existing capabilities, you have a corporate ChangeQuake. The company does not have a new proprietary capability; it just uses its existing proprietary capabilities to produce a new Killer Value Proposition.

A strategic ChangeQuake can occur when a company shifts from one market space to a ten-times-bigger market space. A good example of this arises from one of our portfolio companies, MicroStrategy. This enterprise software company started out addressing the space for data-warehousing, intelligence-gathering software. It is about a $2 billion space. But in 1999, CEO Mike Saylor shifted the company's existing technology to a much bigger and faster growing space: e-commerce intelligence. It is potentially a $25–$30 billion space, and the company is now maintaining its 100 percent a year growth rate in a ten times bigger market opportunity.

Economic ChangeQuakes are economy-wide in nature and affect the entire society. The introduction of the steam engine was an economic ChangeQuake. The economics of the economy changed. Thereafter, navigation on rivers and the distribution of goods were never the same. The introduction of the light bulb was an economic ChangeQuake. Suddenly, night could be turned into day. People could work a second and third shift. People could read after they got home from work. Sleeping and eating patterns changed. Nothing was ever the same.

The new, order-of-magnitude communications capability that converged in 1995–1996 with a new global data sharing capability (TCP/IP), a new way to move data at the speed of light (Dense Wave Division Multiplexing or DWDM), and a new way to view data via HTML and the Netscape browser erupted into an economic ChangeQuake. Together they are changing the economics of most industries through a host of Killer Value Propositions which entrepreneurs are bringing to the market.

Killer Value Propositions

Just because you have a ChangeQuake does not mean investable change is imminent. Massive shifts in customer demand are not caused by ChangeQuakes—they are caused when entrepreneurial companies offer Killer Value Propositions (KVPs)— new, order-of-magnitude improvements in the status quo, or what's known as the "existing value proposition."

It's human nature again. Very few human beings have an inner craving for new technology or lust for new ways of doing things. What most people crave is a clearly superior way to satisfy their insatiable, DNA-encoded emotional hungers and desires.

Marketers worth their salt know that in free-market capitalism, customers only change behavior when they see a new way of doing things that appears much more emotionally satisfying than their current product or service. The end result is that they become emotionally engaged and driven to act and try the new thing.

Marketers understand Killer Value Propositions and emotionally relevant promises because that's what they do—they are in the business of inventing them. As master advertising wizard Roy H. Williams teaches us in his seminal book on marketing, *The Wizard of Ads*, "Intellect and Emotion are partners who do not speak the same language. The intellect finds logic to justify what the emotions have already decided."

Amen, Brother Williams. Truer words have never been spoken about Killer Value Propositions. Remember how you rationalized your first cell phone? "It's for safety." Right.

ChangeQuakes make Killer Value Propositions possible. They are the catalyst for irreversible secular shifts or conversions in customer demand. But ChangeQuakes aren't the final, packaged solutions and promises that mass numbers of people can't emotionally ignore or refuse. In the context of growth investing, where there is smoke (i.e., a ChangeQuake or potentially discontinuous new capability), there is often fire (a new Killer Value Proposition that is created out of the new capability). ChangeWave Investors keep both eyes open for radical new capabilities that may come into an economy or an industry or even a company. When you see one, you may be observing the beginning of an investable transition—a ChangeWave.

ChangeWaves

A *ChangeWave* is a rapidly growing, highly investable secular economic or strategic transition. ChangeWaves are the basis for a "no-brainer" secular growth assumption. Economic Change-Waves can occur at the industry, sector, or macroeconomic levels. We judge an economic ChangeWave "investable" when its rate of its aggregate revenue growth exceeds 90 percent of other industrial sectors in the New Economy. And its projected revenue within 36 to 60 months will exceed $1 billion. Economic ChangeWaves are comprised of industrial sectors and companies that facilitate the secular transition. Strategic ChangeWaves occur at the company level when a shift in leadership or business strategy redefines the value proposition for the business or increases the addressed market by an order of magnitude. When a ChangeWave forms, the potential for discovering one or more monster WaveRider stocks within this wave is very high.

A *Monster ChangeWave* is a macroeconomic or economy-wide secular transition. In the United States economy, we consider a secular macroeconomic transition "monsterish" if it is projected to exceed $1 trillion of revenue over a period of three to five years.

FadWaves and CrashWaves

There is one other kind of investable ChangeWave—I call them *FadWaves*. These FadWaves are caused by a different kind of ChangeQuake and Killer Value Proposition: the emergence of a mass-market consumer fad. The KVP is that the use or purchase of the product is a new way to be cool—and that's a very powerful value proposition and emotional payoff that (for a while) many people can't resist.

Pokémon is the latest example of this highly lucrative but short-lived investable FadWave. One primary beneficiary of the FadWave, FourKids, Inc. (KIDE), rocketed 1,200 percent in 1999 as it rode this wave. Beanie Babies and the premium cigar fad also come to mind as examples.

Of course, the key to playing this game is to identify the FadWave as it is forming and buy the pure-play companies behind the fad and ride them until every magazine and news show is telling everyone about the fad. Then you sell your stock and go the other way—you short the FadWave beneficiary's stock and make money on the way down. We did this in late 1999 with KIDE—shorting the stock at $56 and covering it (meaning buying it back in the open market to return to the broker) at $29. We call that a *CrashWave* play.

SuperSectors, SuperSpaces, and WaveRiders

A *SuperSector* is an industrial sector directly linked to a Monster ChangeWave that has met our growth threshold—growing at a rate more than 500 percent times faster than the S&P 500 growth rate. Operating within a SuperSector are subsectors or spaces linked to the ChangeWave.

A *SuperSpace* is an enabling marketspace within a Super-Sector that meets our growth threshold of eight to ten times the S&P rate of growth. Each SuperSpace consists of an ecosystem of discrete enabling companies.

A company becomes a *WaveRider* when it takes advantage of changes created by a ChangeQuake by offering a Killer Value Proposition in a high growth SuperSector.

So, a quick review.

No ChangeQuake, no Killer Value Proposition. No Killer Value Proposition, no investable ChangeWave or mass transition of people adopting a new way of doing things.

With no ChangeWave, there are no opportunities to invest aggressively in the most strategically advantaged WaveRider companies located within the ChangeWave's enabling sectors and spaces.

And without new WaveRider stocks, there is no rapid new wealth coming into your stock portfolio.

INSTANT REPLAY: HIGHLIGHTS OF PART II

- ChangeWave Investing places the value of a company in the context of the big growth picture and compares it to other companies in the New Economy.

- ChangeWave Investing is a form of modern value investing because it focuses on companies with misunderstood intangible assets that have not been discovered by the institutional investors.

- Institutional growth investors are looking for stocks that produce rapid, consistent results and have an apparent sustainable advantage over their competitors.

- Monster growth comes from killer investable opportunities or ChangeWaves that are at least $1 billion in size and have a growth rate in the top 10 percent of companies in the New Economy.

- There are rules, like universal laws, that govern the behavior of humans and markets.

- ChangeQuakes create an environment for WaveRider companies to develop Killer Value Propositions that spawn ChangeWaves or investable secular transitions. It is these secular transitions or growth stories that create "no-brainer" growth assumptions and "no-brainer" beneficiary sectors, spaces, and WaveRider stocks.

PART III

THE PLAYBOOK:
SCOUTING AND BUYING YOUR
WAVERIDER STOCKS

THE VALUE CHAIN

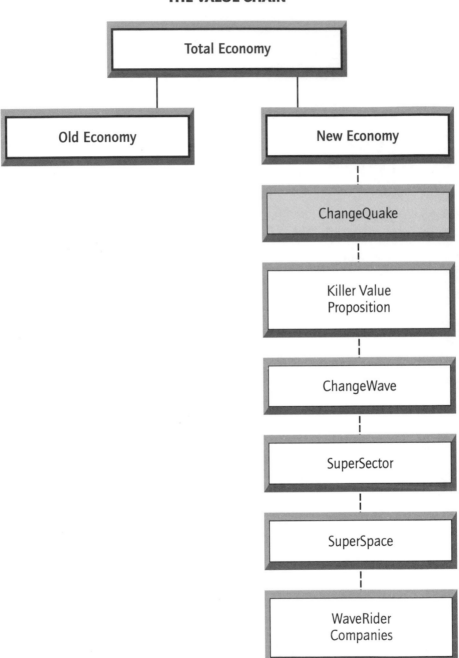

CHAPTER 11

Watching the Richter Scale for the Next Big One

You're now ready for the playbook. It's time to go through the nuts and bolts of the ChangeWave screening process from discovering ChangeQuakes to selecting WaveRider companies for your monster stock portfolio.

Let's start at the very beginning of the chain—the ChangeQuakes.

Discovering ChangeQuakes

How do you find ChangeQuakes? Simply understanding this concept tremendously heightens awareness of ChangeQuakes in everyday work life and business reading. For instance, a Wave-Watcher attended a datacom conference in Zurich last year. The assembly voted on establishing a new high-speed standard protocol from a company called Aware, Inc. as the new core standard for DSL transmissions over copper wire. I got an e-mail from the WaveWatcher disclosing the new capability. It sounded to him like a ChangeQuake had occurred. In a quick follow-up, we discovered that

- Aware held the patented intellectual property (IP).
- The IP was a required piece of the KVP which the DSL companies were about to offer to customers (300 times faster online service).

We bought the stock at around $5 and it zoomed months later to $80 (we ultimately sold it around $60 for a 1,000 percent-plus gain).

This goes to show that everyday reading and experiences are rich veins to tap for the identification of ChangeQuakes if you keep your mind tuned into the "ChangeQuake channel."

Next, I find that New Economy industry newsletters and magazines are very rich sources. The University of Michigan Library has a particularly good list of free industry newsletters at *www.mel.lib.mi.us/business/BU-IPmenu.html.*

The New Economy and technology industry publications like *Red Herring, Business 2.0, The Industry Standard,* as well as *Discovery* magazine and *Science,* are sources of great ChangeQuake leads.

Another way to get news sent to you is to register at *Strategy.com* for the news service. You enter the name of a sector you are checking—say our "Bluetooth" emerging Super-Sector—and you get a daily summary of all the news on that topic from over 20,000 publications. I also use this service to track news on companies and people. It's very powerful—it will notify your digital cell phone, fax, or pager, if you like.

Fred Barbash of the *Washington Post* recommends a wonderful site for ChangeQuake hunting—our own government's National Institute of Standards and Technology (*www.nist.gov*). It regularly identifies the best new research breakthroughs via its Advanced Technology Program.

An easy way to discover new ChangeQuakes is at *ChangeWave.com* in our "Wave Wire" section. We get reports of new potential ChangeQuakes every week, submitted by our WaveWatchers from the far corners of the New Economy. This service is free to registered users and a rich source of leads. We send regular free notification of new ChangeQuakes and Change-Wave formations via fax, e-mail, or pager to registered users.

Aftershocks

An *Aftershock* is a second-generation, ChangeQuake-like improvement in an existing ChangeQuake. A simple example of the power of an Aftershock is Moore's Law regarding the computing power of microprocessors (loosely stated: the power of a semiconductor doubles every 18 months without an increase in cost). New KVPs related to this capability enhancement are easy to predict—because every five years there is an order-of-magnitude improvement in the cost/performance capability of computer chips.

Today, the emergence of XML, or extensible markup language, is a second-generation capability following the HTML ChangeQuake of just a few years ago. HTML is the hypertext markup language that is the standard format for creating web pages. It "tells" Web browsers how to display elements such as text, headlines, and graphics. XML is a younger, smarter cousin of HTML. It's a method of writing programming instructions (called tags) that describe the data itself. In XML, a number is not just a number: the format specifies whether the number represents a price, an invoice, a date, or whatever.

This makes it possible for computers to automatically interpret data and perform all kinds of operations without human intervention. Think about an automaker and a parts supplier. The automaker changes the specs on his order for windshields, and the specs are automatically changed at the parts maker. That change is then automatically made at his windshield foundry—you get the picture.

Aftershocks have a much higher rate of turning into new KVPs and launching profitable ChangeWaves. Usually the overall market is just getting a grip on the ramifications of the initial ChangeQuake and the KVPs that are coming to the marketplace when an Aftershock capability occurs.

THE VALUE CHAIN

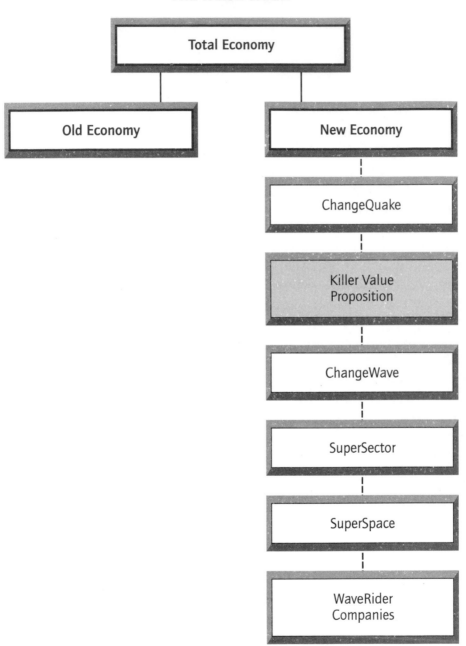

Total Economy

Old Economy

New Economy

ChangeQuake

Killer Value Proposition

ChangeWave

SuperSector

SuperSpace

WaveRider Companies

CHAPTER 12

Finding Riches in Emotional Well Being

Now you know that ChangeQuakes create the opportunity for discontinuous change and the investable event we call a ChangeWave. Someone still has to leverage or use that new capability and turn it into an offer or Killer Value Proposition (KVP) which will give customers such a better, richer emotional payoff they won't be able to refuse. Let's expand on this concept.

The Masses

Obviously, your initial ability to judge a new value proposition as "killer" or merely "incremental" depends on the context of its potential to get mass numbers of people to change or transform their existing behavior. This is the key ingredient to getting in early on the powerful ChangeWaves that form around large market KVPs.

Here's how I separate the wheat from the chaff in KVP land. The basic questions that determine if this is a Killer Value Proposition are "So what?" and "Who cares?" If the first two answers are satisfactory, the final question should be "How many people are there who care?" I ask the following question of every CEO of every company I invest in (and the question is a great one for getting to the bottom of just about any business idea, too):

> *Specifically, what exactly is it that you so uniquely do for people that they find so relevant and indispensable to their emotional well being and so much better than alternatives that they are willing to pay you 120 percent or more of the entire cost of providing the service or product for them?*

Try this at the office, folks—it's a weak-idea killer if I ever saw one.

Emotional Payoff

If the answer I get to this question does not appear to be near an order-of-magnitude improvement in emotional payoff compared to existing services or products, I find the service or product *evolutionary* and not revolutionary. I don't invest in incrementally improved products or services. And if you want monsterish growth, I strongly suggest you don't either.

The hardest answer for tech heads or for nonmarketers to give is the one for the emotional payoff question. *Every product or service delivers an emotional payoff that makes the buyer feel better than alternative propositions.* Every product or service. I don't care if you make radio-frequency chips or sell firewood, there is an emotional payoff people are seeking, and if your product or service seems to be the best way the buyer can afford to satisfy her emotional desire, she will choose you.

The emotional payoff that most business-to-business (B2B) products or service decisions provide is job security and anxiety reduction. Most B2B buyers want predictability or interoperability from their services or products because pre-dictability and proven interoperability make most people feel safer and more secure in their jobs. Or the emotional payoff represents a reduction of work or worry level.

That's why the personal computer didn't take off until IBM launched its version in 1981. Before IBM entered the market, managers of information services were nervous about Apple or Commodore or even Texas Instruments PCs. After IBM unveiled its product, that changed: "Nobody ever got fired for buying IBM."

Killer Value Proposition

Do you want to become a great investment strategist (or marketing strategist for that matter)? First, find the emotional payoff of a new service or product and measure it against the emotional priorities of the people who are the intended market

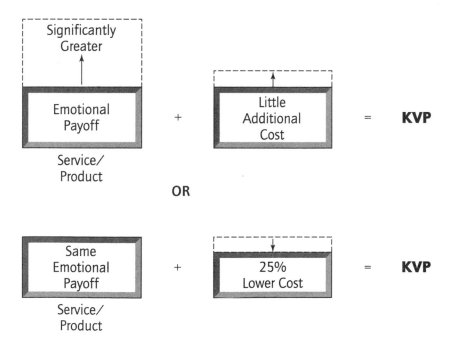

for that product or service. If the service or product delivers a *significantly greater* emotional payoff for relatively *little additional cost* than the alternatives, you have a Killer Value Proposition. This also holds true if the service or product delivers the *same* magnitude of emotional payoff at a significantly *lower* cost (25 percent or more).

The actual value in a service or product that makes people change their purchasing behavior is the cost and personal relevancy of its emotional payoff value versus the cost and degree of emotional payoff provided by alternatives. To understand a product's or service's value proposition, you first have to understand the primary payoff people are seeking when they make a purchase. Are they buying better sleep at night, less worry, more love, less anxiety—what is the primary emotional hunger they are trying to feed?

A product's or service's emotional payoff has to match the highest priority sought by most customers from its use—otherwise few people will buy it. After you've solved this riddle you have to gauge how much people are willing to pay to get the emotional payoff they desire.

Marketing and Selling

Figuring out what emotional payoff people value highest and matching that desire to the primary payoff of a service or product is called marketing. Communicating the Killer Value Proposition and getting people to accept your offer is called selling—please don't confuse the two.

Marketers, Technologists, and Financial Analysts

Great marketers can make great stock strategists and stock pickers. Since the best marketers are great Killer Value Proposition–creators, they are also very good at identifying them. You see, great technologists are great at creating potential

ChangeQuake technological innovations. Great financial analysts are great at analyzing the financial health of a company. But neither is particularly good at the early identification of new Killer Value Propositions entering the marketplace. It takes a great marketer to see a great KVP because a great marketer sees products and services through a lens that only sees desires and emotional payoffs.

THE VALUE CHAIN

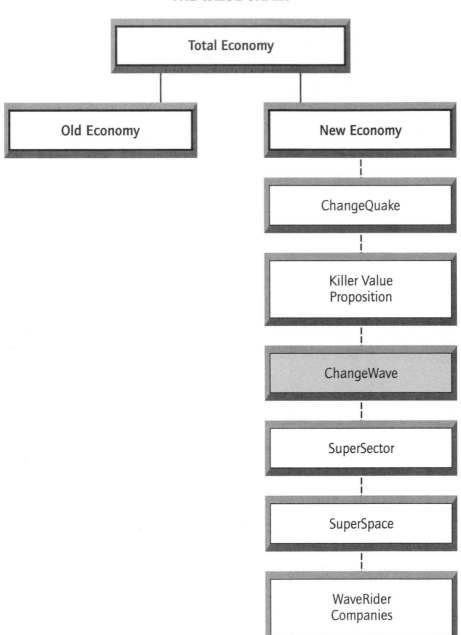

CHAPTER 13

The Four Trillion-Dollar ChangeWaves

As of January 15, 2000, we had identified four trillion-dollar Monster ChangeWaves exploding across the global New Economy.

The Four Biggies Now

Business-to-Me-commerce (B2Me): The trillion-dollar shift from e-commerce to a second-generation "me-centric" intelligent and personalized commerce via *any* media: store, phone, browser, personal digital device, or Web.

Business-to-Business e-commerce (B2B): The multitrillion-dollar shift from analog, client/server, and EDI-based commerce to electronic B2B Digital Direct Interchange within digital, Internet Protocol–based intelligent trading environments.

Virtual Enterprise Genesis: The trillion-dollar conversion from vertically integrated manufacturing and client/server–based processing to "Not-at-All" manufacturing and non-value-adding service e-sourcing delivered over Internet Protocol computing architecture from off-site Application Service Providers.

Broadband InfoGenesis: The trillion-dollar shift from terrestrial narrow-band, separate voice-and-data connectivity to utility-grade understructure (i.e., 99.999 percent reliability and multimillion-user scalability) for the high-speed processing, storage, and delivery of digital, packet-based voice, data, audio, and video information transported down one pipe to anywhere, to any device, all over the world.

If you're not a New Economy professional, you may feel a little lost with some of the New Economy vocabulary. Later in this chapter there is a detailed description of each of the four Monster ChangeWaves.

On Deck

We have a few other trillion-dollar economy-wide shifts on deck, starting with the rapidly approaching Genomics Revolution. Genomics, the study of all the genes in a living organism, is about to transition from the laboratory to the daily practice of medicine. If genomics delivers on its promise, the multitrillion-dollar health care business will shift from a focus on detection and treatment to a process of prediction and prevention. Yes, fortunes will be made riding this Monster ChangeWave, too.

The other Monster ChangeWave in formation is B2G/ G2Me-commerce—business-to-government and government-to-me commerce. With a trillion-plus dollars of state and federal money being spent each year, we are close to the lesson of B2B and B2Me-commerce igniting a similar move in government e-commerce.

The economic impact of the emerged $4–$5 trillion shifts in activity over the next three to five years is unprecedented in the history of peacetime economies. And it is the simultaneous, cumulative effect of these seismic shifts that spawned the New Economy.

Wealth-Creating Waves

Four currently identified Monster ChangeWaves are the secular revenue growth drivers for every investment position we hold in ChangeWave Capital Partners L.P. (a private hedge fund I manage) and every WaveRider stock we own or recommend owning to ChangeWave Investing advisory service subscribers.

So let me explain them.

Business-to-Consumer or "B2Me-Commerce" ChangeWave

Description: The "B2Me-commerce" ChangeWave represents the shift from businesses being in control of the business-to-customer relationship to a second-generation "me-centric" intelligent, personalized e-commerce. The customer is in control of the business relationship, and the relationship is all about the customer's needs and wants. B2Me-commerce means integrating physical and Internet selling channels so seamlessly that consumers can buy with equal ease through a store, catalog, or browser located on any digital device they prefer.

Initial Enabling ChangeQuakes: Internet Protocol and HTML standardization (i.e., the emergence of a standard for global reach of rich data communications via PC); Dense Wave Division Multiplexing (i.e., the new capability of sending trillions of times more data at the speed of light than in the old fiber-optic backbones).

Enabling Aftershocks: XML (a way to share all kinds of data with anyone on any device in real time); third-generation wireless Web connectivity.

◄ ┄┄┄┄┄┄┄┄

Killer Value Proposition: Nordstrom service, Wal-Mart pricing, and 7-11 convenience.

Three-Year Projected Cumulative Annual Growth Rate (CAGR): 100 percent-plus.

Analysis: In 1985, sending one million bits of information from New York to Los Angeles cost about $100. Today that cost is a penny, and it's still dropping. What really happened the day a worldwide standard for information exchange (TCP/IP) met computers doubling in speed/dropping in price every 18 months (Moore's Law) and high-speed fiber-optic cables tripling in capacity every year is that the consumer got the power to take over the marketplace from business. For the first time in the history of commerce, the marketing power in most industries has shifted from the company to the customer. Customer ignorance is no longer a profit center.

B2Me-commerce is shorthand for "high richness–high reach" service. In the Old Economy, richness and reach were inversely proportional to price. To get rich, informed, and personal service anywhere or anytime you desired it, you paid high prices. With broadband Internet and wireless data access eliminating the geographic consideration (reach), and intelligent data-mining and personalization software providing detailed knowledge (informational richness), the Old Economy formula for competitive advantage strategy flies out the window.

B2Me-commerce is much different than first generation e-commerce of just a few years ago. B2Me-commerce is all about Me, not "e." B2Me-commerce is about *me* getting what I want, when I want it, at the price I want it, where I want it— all on *my terms*. It means if I want to go to a store, I want a physical store. If I want to order from my Palm Pilot, I will. Me-commerce is not just online—it's everywhere. B2Me-commerce is the customer's demand for Nordstrom service, 7-11 ubiquity, Domino's timeliness, and K-Mart pricing.

This historic shift means that for companies to continue to prosper in the emerging era of the customer as boss, they, for the very first time in their lives, have to learn how to play the business game by their customers' rules and restructure most of their processes and systems from stem to stern. The B2Me-commerce genie is officially out of the bottle, and it means both individual and business-to-business commerce will never be the same again.

Business-to-Business (B2B) E-Commerce ChangeWave

Description: The "B2B e-commerce" ChangeWave represents the trillion-dollar shift from analog, client/server, and EDI-based commerce to electronic Digital Direct Interchange within digital, Internet Protocol–based intelligent trading ecosystems.

Initial Enabling ChangeQuakes: Internet Protocol and HTML standardization (i.e., the emergence of a global standard for global reach of rich data communications via PC); Dense Wave Division Multiplexing (i.e., the new capability of sending trillions of times more data at the speed of light than in the old fiber-optic backbones).

Enabling Aftershocks: XML (a way to share any kind of data with anybody on any device in real time).

Killer Value Proposition: $1.2 trillion in material, labor, and processing cost savings by 2003.

Three-Year CAGR: 200 percent-plus.

Analysis: B2B e-commerce is the trillion-dollar shift of enterprise information technology from the cost center of a business to a strategic value creator and profit center. B2Me-commerce will hit a behavioral limit or ceiling adoption rate (think about your never-wired friends). Yet, *100 percent* of businesses will adopt intelligent business-to-business e-commerce because it's faster, better, and cheaper. The best analogy is the way business moved from being Telex and first-class-mail–based to being fax-based. Once fax machines became ubiquitous, everybody threw away their Telex—it was a 100 percent conversion. The same will happen with B2B e-commerce. This is why the B2B e-commerce opportunity will in five years be four to five times larger than the B2Me-commerce opportunity.

The Virtual Enterprise ChangeWave

Description: The trillion-dollar shift from vertically integrated manufacturing and client/server–based business processing to "Not-at-All" manufacturing (i.e., built-to-order manufacturing conducted by contract manufacturing services) and high-value-adding-service e-sourcing of business processes delivered over Internet devices.

Initial Enabling ChangeQuakes: Internet Protocol and HTML standardization (i.e., the emergence of a global standard for global reach of rich data communications via PC); Dense Wave Division Multiplexing (i.e., the new capability of sending trillions of times more data at the speed of light than in the old fiber-optic backbones).

Enabling Aftershocks: XML (a way to share all kinds of data with anyone on any device in real time).

Killer Value Proposition: $1 trillion in supply chain, labor, and processing cost savings by 2003.

Three-Year CAGR: 100 percent-plus.

Analysis: The Virtual Enterprise ChangeWave represents the trillion-dollar shift of corporations from vertically integrated or closed enterprises to open enterprises or "extraprises" that only keep "in-house" functions that uniquely and directly create value for customers and shareholders. Virtual enterprises create value for customers from their proprietary intellectual property and speed to market with innovative solutions. They create value for shareholders by marketing and selling their proprietary intellectual property–based solutions at a profit. Any other part of the value creation and delivery chain that does not add distinguishable value to the customer gets outsourced or e-sourced. This shift of corporations focusing exclusively on unique, value-adding competencies and relying on other "core-centered" firms to do what they do best is fundamentally changing the models of most businesses. It represents a transition from "Just-in-Time" manufacturing to "Not-at-All" manufacturing, from in-house supply sourcing/business processing to e-processing and e-sourcing. The key enabling factor is once again the Killer Value Propositions being created by companies harnessing unlimited bandwidth and the worldwide-data communication standard called the Internet.

The Broadband InfoGenesis ChangeWave

Description: The Broadband InfoGenesis ChangeWave is the trillion-dollar shift of the world's communication understructure from nondigital, circuit-switched communications and narrow band connectivity to utility-grade (i.e., 99.999 percent reliability and multimillion-user scalability), digital packet–based voice/data/audio/video pipe to anywhere, to any device, virtually anyplace in the world.

Initial Enabling ChangeQuakes: Internet Protocol and HTML standardization (i.e., the emergence of a global standard for global reach of rich data communications via PC); Dense Wave Division Multiplexing (i.e., the new capability of sending trillions of times more data at the speed of light than in the old fiber-optic backbones); CDMA digital wireless technology.

Coming Aftershocks: Third Generation Wireless Web—a way to deliver wireless broadband Internet access to non-PC Internet appliances.

Killer Value Proposition: 100 times faster connectivity bandwidth, at 10 times lower cost, to any destination by 2002.

Three-Year CAGR: 0.5 percent to 25 percent of all U.S. online households with broadband Internet access by 2003— 5 percent to 75 percent penetration of all businesses.

Analysis: Our first three ChangeWaves require massive increases in telecommunication bandwidth. According to industry experts, more than $1 trillion will be spent over the next five years creating a utility-grade "infranet" or public high-speed fiber-optic Internet core and "wireless fiber" network understructure connecting everyone to everything. A broadband, packet-based public fiber and wireless network will add another 700 million telephone lines, and 500 million wireless subscribers to the 700 million existing lines and 200 million existing wireless subscribers. According to industry experts, twice as much money will be spent on the project than the total undepreciated value of the gear put in place over the last 50 years.

THE VALUE CHAIN

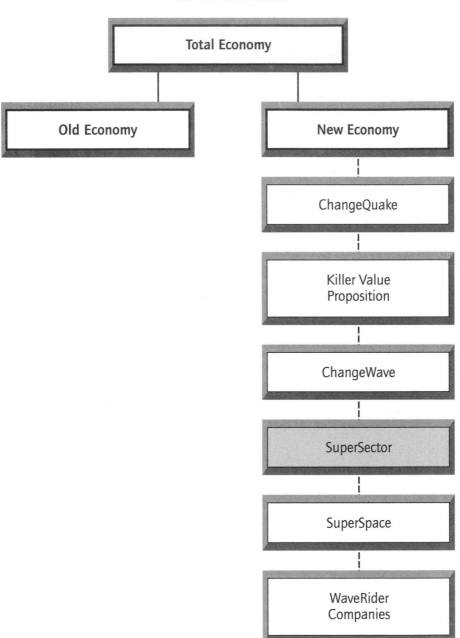

CHAPTER 14

Mapping the Top 10 Growth SuperSectors

Mapping the Waves, Sectors, and Spaces

We've identified the ChangeWaves. We've traced them back to a technological ChangeQuake and identified the Killer Value Propositions that will drive people to change their existing buying behavior en masse to a better, much more fulfilling way of getting what they want.

How do you make money with your discovery? You need a treasure map.

And in ChangeWave Investing, this is called WaveMapping and SpaceMapping. To draw a map to the WaveRider stocks that will dominate their spaces, you have to understand the value chain.

Every ChangeWave formed by a Killer Value Proposition creates a supply chain "ecosystem" or value chain of enabling component industries or sectors. The fastest growing sectors, SuperSectors, have, in turn, an ecosystem of enabling component subsectors as well. And within these subsectors or SuperSpaces are investable companies vying for overall market domination or for domination of significant niches within the marketplace.

Putting together a schematic drawing or map of these interrelationships is what we mean by WaveMapping. The concept is simple, but the execution is not. Effective WaveMapping requires understanding of the nature and components of a ChangeWave. This is why we created *ChangeWave.com* and the ChangeWave Alliance (CWA), to assist you in your mapping efforts.

Quite simply, the more accurate your WaveMap, the better your chances of finding the next monster stock of the New Economy.

CONNECTING THE DOTS

Company

KVP

Enabling technology or service

Customer

We map ChangeWaves by asking the simple question, "What does a company have to buy to deliver the Killer Value Proposition?" For me, the easy way to start mapping is to form a mental picture of a company using the KVP to deliver a product or service. What technological and service pieces are required for the KVP to be delivered? Then I simply "connect the dots" between the most basic component of the enabling product or service and the final dot—the customer.

Making It All Possible

Strategic enablers are technologies or services which make possible order-of-magnitude-improved end solutions. Virtually all product or service solutions in the New Economy are made possible through one or more pivotal technologies or services that, when combined with other existing technologies, make the end-results solution possible. These technologies or services are called "enabling" because without them, companies would not be able to deliver the KVP to customers.

Your PC would not deliver the functionality you treasure without a microprocessor and operating system that work together (enabling technology). You could substitute many components, but without an operating system that's integrated with the brains of your computer, your PC is not able to function.

Owning the proprietary intellectual property behind a key enabling component of a New Economy ChangeWave is the holy grail of commerce. If you own the one piece of the value chain that is critical to an end-user solution, you own a very valuable thing. Just ask QUALCOMM.

Working Backwards

Imagine the strategic links from the infrastructure back end to the customer interface front end. Who sells to whom for you to click your mouse and complete a transaction? Think of these sectors as discrete layers of services or products.

For example, here are the enabling sector layers our map would track for the B2Me-commerce Monster ChangeWave:

- the infrastructure back-end layer
- the connectivity processing layer
- the database layer
- the application layer
- the packet transportation layer
- the end-user interface front end

Now we "sector map" each of these layers. Within each sector layer resides discrete functional sublayers or "spaces." For instance, the database layer of the B2Me-commerce ChangeWave contains multiple spaces.

SECTOR MAP

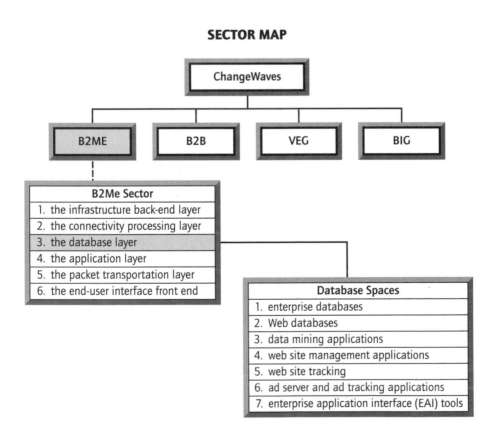

The B2Me-commerce SuperSpace includes:

- enterprise databases
- web databases
- data mining applications
- web site management applications
- web site tracking
- ad server and ad tracking applications
- enterprise application interface (EAI) tools

We rank New Economy sectors by

- Projected Cumulative Annual Growth Rate (CAGR %)
- Addressed Market Opportunity (AMO in $)

The top ten growth sectors based on this ranking we call "SuperSectors." It is from within these SuperSectors that we endeavor to find the next emerging monster growth stocks.

SpaceMapping Made Easy

When you get all the sectors arrayed, and rank them by CAGR and AMO, the top ten ranked become SuperSectors.

So, when you SpaceMap a SuperSector, it's easiest if you select a company that is actually delivering the ChangeWave you're mapping. For instance, if you mapped the "Broadband-to-Home" SuperSector, you'd start at the front end of an application enabled by the sector and work backwards to identify the enabling spaces.

E-Trade SpaceMap

If you SpaceMap the online brokerage sector, think about an online service like E-Trade. How does the investor actually get to the site to click the "buy" button?

How does the page you see at E-Trade get generated? It takes software to connect the Oracle database they keep on their IBM mainframes to their Sun MicroSystems web server. This means using enterprise integration software (EAI). If you go to E-Trade on the Web and look back over its announcements for the past few years, you'll see that BEA Systems is their vendor of choice. BEA Systems has been our EAI E.G.O.D. selection in this SuperSpace for 1999 and has rewarded us with 896 percent return so far this year.

How does your trade get executed? Turns out a company called Knight/Trimark (NITE) does about 75 percent of all the online brokerage clearing in the U.S. We bought NITE at $20 before it shot to $85 as soon as everyone else came to this blinding flash of the obvious.

Next, the page has to be downloaded into your browser—that takes a network. Visualize who owns Internet service pipes across the country—yeah, a company like MCI WorldCom.

Okay, how does WorldCom get the capability or capacity to carry your data? Internet plumbing devices—servers, routers, and switches—and fiber-optic backbones—fiber, amplifiers, etc. The plumbing devices are the products from Cisco and Lucent, and the fiber optics are from companies like JDS Uniphase and SDL, Inc. All 1,000 percent winners for us, too.

Who sells strategic functional components to Cisco and JDS Uniphase? Now your SpaceMap will include the silicon intellectual property owners or chip makers like PMC-Sierra and optical lenses from Optical Coating, Inc. Both stocks again averaging over 750 percent appreciation for us since early 1999.

Get the idea? It's sort of like playing the Kevin Bacon game—you know, naming an actor and then linking the actor through his or her movie roles and co-stars until you get to a movie with Kevin Bacon.

If you're feeling a little lost here, remember, you can always go to *ChangeWave.com* and start investigating a company's value chain with a portfolio manager. Or you can go to *finance.Yahoo.com* and use their portfolio manager. Use *Google.com*, too, to search under key phrases like "E-Trade partnerships" or "strategic alliances."

Your surfing could literally earn you hundreds of thousands in profits—and keep your spouse off your back for being on the computer too long.

Top 10 SuperSectors

ChangeWave Investing has mapped the four Monster Change-Waves into more than 100 different industrial sectors and identified those sectors which can meet our growth threshold—growing at a rate more than ten times faster than the S&P 500 growth rate. As of January 15, 2000, the Top 10 Super-Sectors (ranked by rate of 2000–2003 CAGR and projected annual sector revenue in 2003) were

1. optical Internet infrastructure and services
2. wireless Internet infrastructure and services
3. B2Me-commerce enterprise software
4. B2B e-commerce enterprise software
5. data storage bandwidth infrastructure
6. e-service provision and application services
7. digital services value-added infrastructure and services
8. e-process/e-sourcing infrastructure and services
9. non-PC computing
10. broadband-to-home

Here's a short description of these SuperSectors 2000:

1. **Optical Internet Infrastructure and Services:** Changing the Internet backbone from part-optical/part-electronic to full-optical transmission is a $500 billion transition over the next 36 to 60 months.
2. **Third Generation (3G) Wireless Internet Infrastructure and Services:** From virtually nothing in 1998, knowledge workers will spend more than $8 billion on wireless data services by

2003. 3G service will be launched in Japan in early 2000, in Europe in 2001, and in the U.S. by 2002.

3. **B2Me-Commerce Enterprise Software and Services:** Forrester Research forecasts that the market for business-to-me commerce will grow to from $20 billion in 1999 to over $100 billion by 2003.

4. **B2B E-Commerce Enterprise Software and Services:** Forrester Research forecasts that the market for business-to-business e-commerce will grow to $251 billion next year and to $1.4 trillion by 2003. By 2002, conducting business online will save companies around the world an estimated $1.25 trillion, according to a report by the Giga Information Group. This compares to a total savings of $17.6 billion in 1998.

5. **Data Storage Bandwidth Infrastructure:** The B2B and B2Me-commerce explosion is fueling a 200 percent annual increase in data storage. Gartner Group estimates more than 75 percent of enterprise hardware expenditures will be related to data storage by 2003.

6. **E-Services Provision and Application Services:** International Data Group projects the market for Internet-delivered services to grow from $7.8 billion in 1998 to $78.5 billion in 2003. The hottest part of this sector is the Application Service Provider and Hosting space, growing at more than 200 percent annually.

7. **Enhanced Digital Services Infrastructure and Services:** This sector represents the services that bandwidth providers can add. Services include virtual private networking, Internet telephony, streaming applications, e-mail–enhanced services such as registered e-mail, and digital services like voice mail and video conferencing.

8. **E-Process/E-Sourcing Infrastructure and Services:** This segment will grow more than 70 percent CAGR from $100 billion in 1998 to $400 billion in 2003. E-services include all enterprise manufacturing, supply-chain management, and business processes except for selling, marketing, and proprietary intellectual property research and development. Outsourced contract electronic manufacturing alone will grow from $90 billion in 1998 to more than $200 billion in 2001.

9. **Non-PC Computing:** So-called "Net appliances" will grow from about 5 million devices to over 65 million by 2003. This segment includes smart phones, personal digital devices like the Palm Pilot, and digital TV set-top boxes.

10. **Broadband-to-Home:** 700,000 residential broadband service subscribers are projected to grow to 14.7 million by 2003. Options include Digital Subscriber Lines (DSL), cable modems, data satellite networking, and fixed wireless or "wireless cable."

Looking Forward

At *ChangeWave.com* we are tracking literally dozens of emerging SuperSpaces. New industries like

- **E-Learning:** Educational services via the computer on the Internet. Addressing a $100 billion opportunity, e-learning software and services are just about ready for prime-time.

- **Wireless Monitoring (Telemetry):** Wireless monitoring of things like parking meters and utility meters is poised to begin its rise to a $1 billion-plus annual industry from less than $200 million today.

- **Satellite Radio:** In late 2000 commuters and long-haul drivers will be offered the option of the equivalent of satellite TV in their cars—100 channels of mostly ad-free radio.
- **High Definition Digital Television:** By 2002, the FCC has mandated that everyone in the United States must have access to digital television—that's quite a Regulatory ChangeQuake, I'd say. Now someone has to put together a Killer Value Proposition like satellite TV in order to create a ChangeWave.
- **Photonic Switching:** Data traveling as laser light impulses over fiber-optic cables. Why convert light to electrons when you can skip the process and just switch light? This emerging KVP will lower the cost of telecommunications by orders of magnitude.

One thing is certain: I can guarentee that our *next* monster growth companies will come from within sectors that barely exist today.

THE VALUE CHAIN

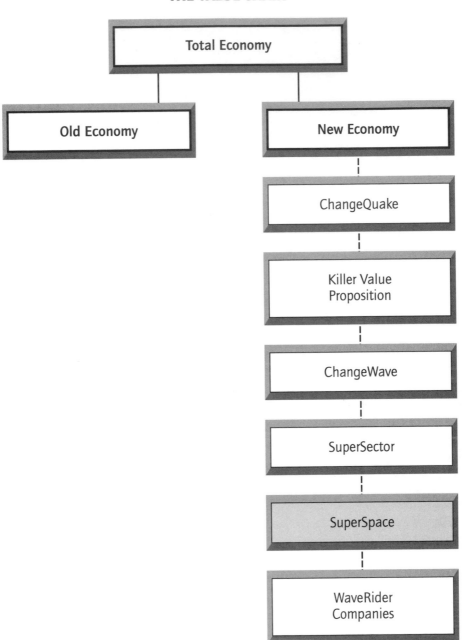

CHAPTER 15

Screening for Big Payoff SuperSpaces

Now we tighten our strategic screen down to less than 10 percent of all the discrete industry categories or spaces operating within our Top 10 SuperSectors of the global economy.

Within each New Economy industry are subsectors or industrial categories we call "spaces"—a supporting or enabling subsector industry within a New Economy sector. It is from within these New Economy subsectors or spaces that the monster growth stocks we call "WaveRider" stocks are found.

The Big Question

To determine which spaces to research, we take these Top 10 SuperSectors and ask the question, "Which multibillion-dollar spaces within these enabling sectors are best positioned to capture the cascading effect of the trillion-dollar Change-Waves and turn them into billions of dollars of new, rapid, and sustainable revenue growth and profits?"

SuperSpace Criteria

We look for a SuperSpace that

- is projected to grow at least eight to ten times faster than the overall economy for the next 36 to 60 months;
- holds an enabling control position within the value chain of a secular growth SuperSector that's riding a trillion-dollar ChangeWave; or
- directly provides a Killer Value Proposition to multi-billion-dollar markets;
- if an emerging SuperSpace, is projected to become a billion-dollar industry in the next 60 months;
- if an emerged SuperSpace, is projected to become a multibillion-dollar industry in the next 60 months.

Discovering the SuperSpaces

When you list the companies that provide services or products in the Top 10 SuperSectors (see chapter 14), you see groups of companies that compete against each other within the sector. As you cluster the companies within the discrete subsectors of a sector, you now have spaces and the combatants within the space. When you rank all those spaces identified on your sector SpaceMaps by CAGR, addressed market opportunity, and the average gross profit margin, the top 10 percent of those spaces become SuperSpaces.

For example, in the e-commerce enterprise software Super-Sector, the companies by subsector or space are

E-purchasing software space
- Ariba
- Commerce One
- Clarus
- Concur Technologies

E-commerce platform software space

- BroadVision
- Vignette
- Art Technology Group
- Allaire

E-customer service software space

- Silknet Software
- Kana Communications
- eGain
- Mustang.com

As you rank these spaces by CAGR, AMO, and GPM, you will discover that e-purchasing software space ranks highest. Thus, it is no coincidence that the two leaders of that space, Ariba and Commerce One, are among the best performing stocks of 1999.

TOP 2000 SUPERSPACES

E-Marketing Infrastructure and Services
Market Size: To $31 billion in 2003, from $6.2 billion in 1998
Projected CAGR: 60 percent

Application Service Provider Software
Market Size: To $6.4 billion in 2002, from $100 million in 1998
Projected CAGR: 115 percent

B2Me/B2B E-Business Enterprise Platform Software
Market Size: To $5.1 billion in 2002, from $200 million in 1998
Projected CAGR: 98 percent

E-Procurement Infrastructure and Services
Market Size: To $8.5 billion in 2003, from $187 million in 1998
Projected CAGR: 134 percent

TOP 2000 SUPERSPACES (continued)

Internet Application Integration
Market Size: To $1.5 billion in 2003, from $265 million in 1998
Projected CAGR: 67 percent

Electronic Messaging Infrastructure and Services
Market Size: To $2 billion in 2003, from $110 million in 1998
Projected CAGR: 201 percent

Web Application Server Software
Market Size: To $2 billion in 2003, from $400 million in 1998
Projected CAGR: 75 percent

Network Storage Appliances
Market Size: To $1.5 billion in 2003, from $265 million in 1998
Projected CAGR: 67 percent

E-Customer Relationship Management Software
Market Size: To $7.5 billion in 2003, from $200 million in 1998
Projected CAGR: 145 percent

Seven Functional Categories

SuperSpaces that directly enable New Economy SuperSectors contribute to seven basic categories. Here are the seven Super-Spaces with their functional uses:

1. **Enabling Intellectual Property (IP) Licensor:** These companies create and license enabling core technology for component companies in return for royalties and services. ARM Holdings is a good example of a company dominating this kind of space in the communications semiconductor sector.

2. **Enabling Understructure:** You don't normally see these components, but what I call the understructure

are the parts that make the infrastructure do its magic. Think of enabling understructure as what you'd see if you opened up your satellite dish, cable box, or PC at home. Think Intel Inside.

3. **Enabling Infrastructure**: The basic facilities, services, applications, and end-user components needed for the functioning of a system or delivery of a service. Think Cisco routers or Oracle databases.

4. **Direct/Indirect Solution Provider:** A service delivered to consumers or businesses as an end result or solution of a ChangeWave. Think AOL or Charles Schwab.

5. **Infrastructure Service Provider:** An industry that delivers enabling infrastructure as a service. Think Exodus Communication and Web-hosting.

6. **End-User Interface:** When the Killer Value Proposition for a ChangeWave is a product. Think personal digital appliances or cell phones.

7. **Pilot Fish Beneficiary:** These spaces include companies that primarily earn their living supporting other companies within the six primary spaces. We call them "pilot fish" because like the pilot fish that swim near their host sharks, these spaces live and die with the success of their host space.

SuperSpace Pilot Fish Companies

The final category or layer residing within a SuperSpace value chain is what I call the pilot fish layer. Just like the fish, these companies live with their big shark host and thrive as the host does. They provide an integral component or service to a fast-growing subsector of the SuperSpace or to a key enabling company within the SuperSpace value chain. These pilot fish companies often are missed by inexperienced investors and can be excellent movers. Because of the rapid secular growth rate of the SuperSpace, these strategic enabling companies are locked in for rapid growth, too. A rising tide *does* raise all boats.

An example of how I used this technique to make $60,000 in a few days is a company called Tanisys Technologies, Inc. (TNSU). In researching the PlayStation II SuperSpace and Rambus in particular, I had read a press release about a company that was the only one to introduce memory testing equipment for the Rambus memory chip. Without testing, the chips won't ship.

The company was selling for less than 37 cents at the time. We put a buy-stop on the stock (i.e., an order that in effect says if the stock goes up past a certain price, buy it) at 40 cents. Well, the day that Sony PlayStation announced that Rambus was indeed shipping tons of its proprietary memory chips for the first PlayStation II's, the stock ran to $1.75. We immediately took profits and let it fall back to $1, then we repurchased and waited for the good news to start coming from the company.

I remember when oil drilling was a high-growth industry, there was a dominant company supplying tubing—Maverick Tube. Same thing—bought stock at $2 and sold for $20. Some investors call these "cousin stocks," but I like the pilot fish analogy.

I always look at the press releases for primary value-chain companies and check for pilot fish companies—and I suggest you do, too. They can be at least as lucrative as the monster-stock-to-be you are stalking in the first place.

Orphan ChangeWave SuperSector

Not every SuperSector we invest in is a direct descendant of a Monster ChangeWave. Hence it is called an "orphan" because it does not originate from a Monster ChangeWave. Sometimes an orphan ChangeWave's growth rate is great enough at the sector or industry level to be worthy of further research and investment.

A good example of an orphan SuperSpace is the Sony PlayStation II ChangeWave. With 71 million (one-in-four American homes) PlayStation I machines about to be upgraded to the Killer Value Proposition called PlayStation II in 2000–2001 (and trust me—once you use it, you will never want your old PlayStation again), we have a rapid, multibillion-dollar transition about to take place.

When you SpaceMap the PlayStation industry value chain, you come up with a few non–pure plays (Sony, LSI Logic) and a few pure plays—like Rambus (high speed memory chips will account for 50 percent-plus of Rambus's revenues over the next 24 months) and Electronic Arts (50 percent-plus of revenues come from PlayStation).

Both companies made great WaveRider candidates. But Rambus went on to appreciate 400 percent for us in 30 days!

Pure Play

"Pure play" means that the company generates most if not all of its revenue from a single service or product of a SuperSpace. Wall Street does not reward companies who are half-in, half-out of an acknowledged SuperSpace.

The logic is simple. In the investment game, it's difficult enough to carve out a winning SuperSpace. When one becomes commonly acknowledged, investors want to get paid for their acumen. And the way you get paid is to own the leader or leading companies that derive a majority of their revenues from this now-obvious big secular growth space.

Companies that sell in many market spaces also have a hard time getting and keeping their competitive advantage—too many competitors and not enough firepower to ward off all of them. So we limit our emerging ChangeWave draft universes to companies which are considered a pure play in the

SuperSpace that we worked so hard to figure out was going to be hot.

SpaceMapping Worksheet Instructions

It usually takes less than an hour or so, depending on how complex the SuperSector is, to complete a SpaceMap. All you need is an Internet connection to *Google.com, finance.Yahoo.com,* and a little focused curiosity. It's kinda fun—you're solving a puzzle that literally can make you rich!

Before you start, you may want to walk through the E-Trade example in chapter 14 again.

To begin, list the enabling and solution/application–providing companies you find associated with the SuperSector in your searches. Next, check which of the seven functional categories (see pages 110 and 111) each of the companies fit into.

Then you determine if each of the companies is a pilot fish company or a pure play. Go to your favorite company research site (*Hoovers.com, dowjones.com, finance.Yahoo.com,* etc.) and try to separate the pure plays from the mixed revenue stream businesses. When you have the pure plays defined, do a little more digging to see how they rank in their subsector. Unless the SuperSpace is just emerging (in which case it pays to buy all of the 15 percent-plus market-share players, then wait to see who becomes dominant. You only want the number one and number two players.

And relax—we maintain many of these SuperSpace value-chain charts at *ChangeWave.com*. So you may be just a click away from finding a few potential monster stocks.

Ranking Your Potential SuperSpaces

Once you have identified and mapped several spaces, you gotta choose which ones you are going to play.

Technically, we rank a SuperSpace by

- Growth—its three-year CAGR ranking (1st to 99th percentile)
- Market size—its addressed market size rating
- Average Gross Profit Margin—money after paying cost of goods or services
- Performance—its previous 90-day and 180-day performance track record to date

Growth

Quick review: A 99th percentile ranking means the Super-Spaces' projected 36-month CAGR is greater than 99 percent of all industrial spaces tracked at *ChangeWave.com*. In other words, in the top 1 percent. My advice is to stick with Super-Spaces rated 90 or better.

Market Size

Addressed market opportunity (AMO) index is a rating of all the SuperSpaces identified and tracked in the *Change-Wave.com* emerging and emerged SuperSpace database. The average addressed market size is 1.00 on the index—at twice the average it would be rated 2.00.

I use the addressed market opportunity index as a tie breaker many times. When I have numerous SuperSpaces in the same general rate of secular growth rating, I tend to favor the ones with the largest addressed market, particularly if it is in one of my favorite common-thread enabler SuperSpaces (one that provides an essential, pivotal component throughout the New Economy). When a dominant leader or platform emerges within these SuperSpaces, you have a great candidate for a monster stock, à la VeriSign, Checkpoint Systems, QUALCOMM, Exodus, BEA Systems, TIBCO Software, etc.

Gross Profit Margin

A company with a gross profit margin less than 50 percent does not make it on our team. Our usual cut-off is 70 percent or higher—and many of our WaveRider companies earn 80 percent gross margins.

Performance

The other "tell" you are looking for is actual performance (how the space is performing versus other spaces). Many times a pattern emerges with certain SuperSpaces—they are leaving the other spaces in the dust. A good place to concentrate your buying.

SPACEMAPPING WORKSHEET

SuperSector: Value-Chain Companies	FUNCTIONAL CATAGORIES – Choose one								Pilot Fish Beneficiary	Pure Play?
	Enabling IP Licensor	Enabling Understructure	Enabling Infrastructure	Direct-/Indirect Solution Provider	Infrastructure Service Provider	End-User Interface				
1.										
2.										
3.										
4.										
5.										
6.										
7.										
8.										
9.										
10.										
11.										
12.										
13.										
14.										
15.										

THE VALUE CHAIN

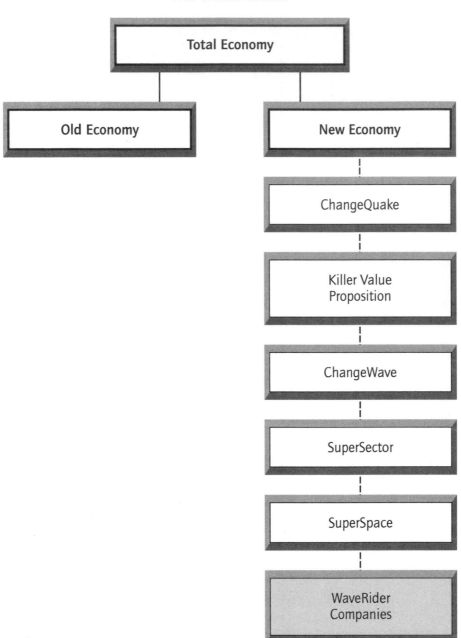

CHAPTER 16

Making Your Draft List of Big Idea Companies

Okay, we're almost home. We made the first strategic screen by eliminating Old Economy companies. Next we identified the four trillion-dollar Monster ChangeWaves. We sector-mapped these huge secular economic shifts to identify the fastest growing industries with the biggest markets and Spacemapped the sectors for the top SuperSpaces.

Now—which companies within the top SuperSpaces do you invest in?

As in professional sports, in ChangeWave Investing, your stocks are your "players." Unlike the real world, on fantasy sports teams you can "draft" any player (stock) you want—that is if you have the money. But like the real world, you are investing real money.

Which League?

In ChangeWave Investing you "draft" your stocks from within the very small and elite universe of growth stocks that have made it through your screening process. Your first order of business is to decide which "league" or risk/reward category you want to play—i.e., which type of stocks you are comfortable owning. This decision is based upon your tolerance for risk and your goals for your aggressive growth portfolio.

Risk and Reward

We organize industries into three major groupings according to the sector's level of development. The difference in these groups or "leagues" is the trade-off in risk and reward.

Emerging Sector—Highest Risk, Highest Return

The highest risk, highest potential short-term-reward stocks come from the emerging sector group league. We know when emerging groups become discovered and thus "emerge," the dominant stocks get hit with the fire hose of Wall Street liquidity and soak up the gains. The risk is whether or not the space will live up to its potential or get ignored. If the industry fails to grow or gets little attention, stocks in this group languish. The emerging HDTV SuperSpace comes to mind as the most recent example of an emerging growth area stuck in neutral.

Emerged Sector—Higher Risk, Higher Return

The emerged group is filled with industries that have been discovered. You know this by the fact that the stocks within these sectors have moved up and are getting media coverage. In this league, your buying entry point is more important. But many of our monster stocks have come from the emerged group because they were still fighting out who was going to become the dominant player—and when they won they blew up in price tenfold. The earlier the buy is made, the greater the upside—and the risk.

Classic Growth—Safest, Most Consistent

The stocks with the safest, most consistent long-term growth are the companies that are the game-over dominators reigning supreme over the widely acknowledged "classic" secular growth sector. For example, everybody now knows that the growth of the World Wide Web traffic is doubling every 100 days or so. The industry that most directly benefits from this growth is the networking sector. Within this group are the classic growth spaces—networking equipment hardware and fiber-optic networking. Cisco and JDS Uniphase are perhaps the best examples of game-over dominators within these respective classic growth SuperSpaces.

We at *ChangeWave.com* spend our effort researching and identifying the *next* monster stocks that are going to come from the emerging or emerged groups. There's already plenty of information out there about the classic growth stocks.

Tie Breaker—Mission Critical Common-Thread Enablers

When a SuperSpace provides enabling components or infrastructure in multiple New Economy sectors, we call it a "mission critical" common-thread enabler. These are "must have" or locked-in enabling pieces. If you are trying to make a choice among several stocks on your draft list, go with the common-thread enabler every time. They're great tie breakers because they make money from virtually everyone in the New Economy.

Mission critical common-thread enabler companies that have a shot at dominating their enabling space are the most sought-after stocks because of the No-Brainer Logic Rule.

Remember? All things being equal, the technology growth stock everyone wants to own is the one with the simplest no-brainer secular growth logic to understand—the "sound bite." I call these companies "mission critical" stocks—i.e., their intellectual property is critical to the continuation of Monster ChangeWaves. Microsoft turned its computer operating system into a mission critical element of PC computing, and you know what happened after that.

Everybody understands that when a company corners or locks in the market for a mission critical element of a Monster ChangeWave, that company explodes in value. This is why we especially prefer dominant common-thread enabler companies like VeriSign (VRSN)—the dominant company enabling web sites to authenticate users. The stock's up 1,200 percent for us since it became an emerging game-over dominator stock in 1998. It's mission critical. No authentication, no Me-commerce. No Me-commerce, no trillion-dollar ChangeWave.

Find a company that has a chance to become a mission critical, intellectual property–based technopoly that everyone in a Monster ChangeWave has to use, and you have a very special WaveRider company.

Setting Up Your Draft Universe

I personally arrange my draft universe by SuperSpace. This way I get to evaluate how each SuperSpace universe of E.G.O.D. and G.O.D. stocks are performing in relation to the other SuperSpaces I am considering. When one set of Super-Space stocks is consistently outperforming the others, I tend to focus on new stock picks from the outperforming SuperSpace.

The reason this works so well is that very few investors (other than fellow WaveWatchers) aggregate their watch stocks this way. Many times the stocks within our SuperSpaces greatly outperform the generic industry sectors they are listed within—which can be a very profitable trend that many investors miss. For instance, this year while the Enterprise Software sector was hot, MicroStrategy (MSTR), which we linked within the B2Me and B2B enterprise software SuperSpaces, outperformed its less-focused competitors. It was much easier to see why when one realized that MSTR was a pivotal enabling technology in *two* top 90 percent growing Super-Spaces, not just one reasonably hot sector.

Identifying WaveRider Prospects

When you discover a new emerging SuperSpace or want to get into an existing emerged SuperSpace, but don't know enough about the space to identify the emerging or emerged WaveRider candidates, my best advice is to find the space's

- Newsletters
- Trade Associations
- Trade Magazines
- Conferences
- Consultants
- Industry Experts

Virtually all the pure-play E.G.O.D. and G.O.D. players in their industry will be mentioned in these media sources.

Where can you find these? On the Web, of course. Just search under the name of the industry category or space's name, and you will find all of these resources in a few minutes. I personally favor *Google.com*, *NorthernLight.com*, *Ask.com*, and *MetaCrawler.com*. They always deliver finer-grained results.

If your exciting SuperSpace doesn't have a newsletter, trade association, trade magazine, conference, or consultant, then you don't have an industry. The existence of an information infrastructure is the first clue to determine if an emerging SuperSpace is ready to be discovered.

Once you have your list of players, separate the private companies from public ones, and eliminate the non-pure-play companies. Although this Web searching takes some work, it is time well invested.

Alternatively, you can check *ChangeWave.com* to see if we are already following your SuperSpace. Many times we will have already set up an Industrial Intelligence Panel within the

ChangeWave Alliance and done most of the work for you. As an open souce investing site most of our research and information on the industry are available at no charge. If your SuperSpace isn't in our database, you can e-mail us at *research@ChangeWave.com* and request us to research it. If the space meets our criteria, we'll recruit an Industrial Intelligence Panel of industry professionals and start building a database on the space.

Whether you are on your own or use *ChangeWave.com*, the Internet empowers all ChangeWave Investing practitioners to build their WaveRider prospect lists in a very efficient manner.

Draft Checklist

Here's a checklist for you to use when building your list "draft" companies:

- In the emerging and the emerged sectors, go for the emerging game-over dominator companies (E.G.O.D.);
- In the classic growth group, go for the game-over dominator (G.O.D.);
- Go with the pure plays;
- And, when you need a tie breaker, go with the mission critical common-thread enabler companies.

THE VALUE CHAIN

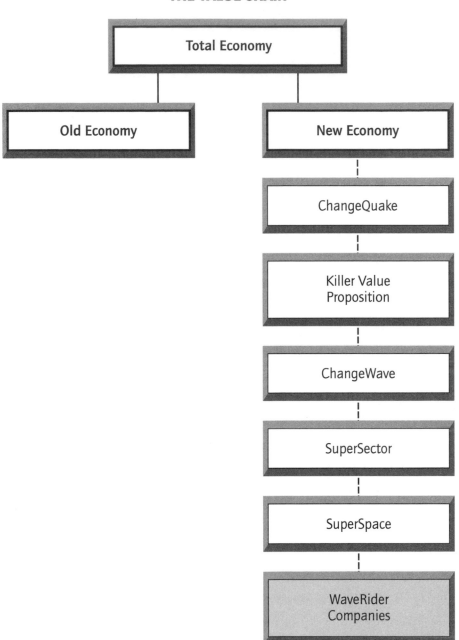

CHAPTER 17

Doing Your Homework on the WaveRiders

You're now ready to thoroughly check out your SuperSpace investment thesis. I call your investment thesis a Big Investment Idea, because most investors I know don't think of themselves as people who come up with an "investment thesis."

What the drafting process does for you is force you to put your investment thesis in context with the other SuperSpaces in the New Economy: why is your Big Investment Idea going to be attractive versus alternative spaces? If your SuperSpace can't be competitive with other areas in the market, you shouldn't be wasting time buying stocks with it.

Make Sure—Check Out the Competition

SuperSpaces and their pure-play WaveRider stocks do not exist in a vacuum—and neither should your investments. Before you put your hard-earned money into what you think is a great growth stock opportunity, shouldn't you be able to make a case as to why you believe it is?

Java 2.0

Let's use the recent introduction of the Java 2.0 Enterprise Edition from Sun Microsystems as an example. Java 2EE, as it is known, is rapidly gaining market share and is in contention to become the dominant standard for the enterprise-wide Internet computing sector in medium to large-size companies. The superior flexibility of this platform and its rapid growth (200 percent-plus in 1999) makes J2EE a SuperSpace for 2000. The strategic fundamentals are that companies are leaving client/server environments and transitioning to Internet protocol computing via the J2EE platform. The Killer Value Proposition is that J2EE allows companies to get their legacy systems into an e-commerce platform 50 percent faster and cheaper than reconfiguring them from scratch.

The Big Investment Idea for this SuperSpace is to invest in the pure-play Java-centric application server software and Java application infrastructure players. The emerging game-over dominators in this SuperSpace are

- BEA Systems: Internet application integration software (BEAS)
- Bluestone Software: Java-centric application server software (BLSW)
- SilverStream Software: Java-centric application server software (SSSW)

Your WaveRider "Draft" Worksheet

So you're bullish on a SuperSpace; you've got a Big Investment Idea. Now you need to buy the pure-play emerging game-over dominator market leader/co-leaders of that space to profit from your insight.

I fill out a "draft" worksheet for every stock I buy—and I strongly suggest you do, too. Because it is this very process that allows ChangeWave investors to compare their Big Investment Ideas in context with the rest of the opportunities available for their portfolio dollar.

You can create your own WaveRider Worksheet from the one in the book, but the easiest way to complete this worksheet is to download the file from *ChangeWave.com*. Or you can go to the site, complete your worksheet, and print it out. All the research and data you need to complete this worksheet should be available at *ChangeWave.com* or are literally one link away.

Makes and Saves You Money

The best advice I can give you on how to improve your aggressive growth investment results is to not skip this part of your investing protocol. This is the part that makes you (and saves you) the most money. If you can take the risk, and losing a quick 10 to 20 grand is no big deal, you can skip this section. Think of your homework as an insurance policy. Why?

1. It forces you to articulate and think through just what the hell you are doing—this point alone could double your investment returns. In just one page, you're boiling down your strategic fundamentals assumptions and your business fundamentals assumptions and analysis into an investment hypothesis. Many times I find this process alone either (a) keeps me from making a mistake and buying someone else's problem, or (b) enhances my conviction to the point that I buy more shares than I was planning to and add to my profits.

2. The worksheet gives you a record of your thinking that you can use to do your quarterly and end-of-year reviews of your results and as a backup for your "Investing Diary." I refer to these "draft"

worksheets often—particularly when I add to my Investing Diary. If you don't have one, my strong advice is to start keeping a running diary of patterns you observe in your stocks and spaces, as well as chronicling your assumptions and trades. This will add 10 to 30 percent to your profits every year—I promise. Every six months or so, I review every buy and sell ticket I have, to revisit my successes and my failures. Most of the ChangeWave Investing process was developed through this post facto analysis.

3. Your draft worksheets also serve as a strong dose of courage when the schizophrenic capital markets convulse into a "ChangeStorm/Market Meltdown" and your precious WaveRider company is taking a stomach-lurching beating. I revisit my WaveRider draft worksheets during every Market Meltdown. In fact, my advice is to go to your local office supply store and buy a three-ring binder and an A-to-Z index. I simply file my worksheets alphabetically by company name and keep them near my computer for reference and security.

4. Denial is not a river in Egypt—it's you kidding yourself about how great your stock picking is. Your investment worksheets don't lie—they tell the exact story of where your assumptions are right on and where you are missing something. A little self-honesty has made me a much better stock picker.

The following two pages provide a version of the worksheet:

WAVERIDER WORKSHEET

Date: _____

Company's Name: _____ **Stock Symbol:** _____

The League and The Play: _____

The Blinding Flash of the Not-Yet-Obvious (if this is an emerging SuperSpace) or The Blinding Flash of the Obvious

Growth Assumption: _____

My Big Investment Idea: _____

The Payoff Stock: _____ One-Year Price Target: $ _____

Primary ChangeQuake: _____

Contributing Aftershock(s): _____

The Buyer and The Addressed Market Opportunity: _____

Killer Value Proposition: _____

52Wk High/52Wk Low: _____ **50-Day MA/200-Day MA:** _____

Float: _____ **TTM Sales Growth:** _____ **TTM Earnings Growth:** _____

Relative Price/Earnings/Group Strength: _____ /_____ /_____

ChangeWave Strategic Fundamentals

Monster ChangeWave(s): _____

SuperSector: _____ Market Today/2003: _____ CAGR %: _____

SuperSpace Fundamentals

Name of Superspace: _____

SuperSpace Type: _____ SuperSpace Ranking: _____ Market Today/2003: _____ CAGR %: _____

WaveRider Intellectual Property (IP) Category: _____

WAVERIDER WORKSHEET (continued)

The Corporate WaveRating

5 Waves = 9 points. Excellent; as good as it gets.

4 Waves = 7 points. Very good, but not among the best you've ever seen.

3 Waves = 5 points. Nothing special; average.

2 Waves = 3 points. Lacking; below par.

1 Wave = 1 point. Worthless.

1) Intellectual Property (IP) Rating: _____

7) Corporate Culture Rating: _____

2) Corporate Vision Rating: _____

8) Sales Team/Sales Power Rating: _____

3) CEO Maverick Rating: _____

9) Strategic Alliances/Ecosystem Rating: _____

4) COO Execution Rating: _____

10) Killer Value Proposition Rating: _____

5) CFO Earnings Management Rating: _____

11) Wall Street/Media Sponsorship Rating: _____

6) Market-Share Position Rating: _____

Total Wave Rating Score: _____ Addressed Market Opportunity Index: _____ Avg. Gross Profit Margin: _____

A) Space Growth Rating:_____ B) Wave Rating: _____ C) Avg. IBD Score: _____

Total WaveRider Draft Score: (A+B+C) _____

Technical Fundamentals:_____ Average Volume: _____ Today's Volumne:_____

1) Speculative Buy Price (above 50-day average but below 52-week high) $_____

2) Break-out Buy Price (less than 5% over 52-week high) $ _____

3) Quick Cut Sell Price (8–10% below buy price) $ _____

4) Secondary Upgrade Price: $_____ by_____ (20% up move within 4–6 weeks of purchase on higher volume)

5) Double-Up Price: $_____ by_____ (breakthrough of 52-week high on higher volume or 20% higher move from secondary upgrade price)

Notes about Your Worksheet

Most of this data is available to registered users of *Change-Wave.com*. More important, if you don't find the data you need to complete a WaveRider draft worksheet, just e-mail us at *research@ChangeWave.com* and ask us to help. We'll e-mail back your answer as quickly as possible.

Best of all, this research service is free—that's what open source investment research is all about. And your inquiry helps *all* ChangeWave investors stay ahead of the curve on emerging potential SuperSpaces and WaveRider companies. So don't be shy!

Worksheet Fields

Company Symbol: _____

The League and the Play: Decide what kind of investment play this is. An emerging SuperSpace E.G.O.D. play? Or a G.O.D. play in an emerged SuperSpace?

The Blinding Flash of the Not-Yet-Obvious (for an emerging SuperSpace): What new secular ChangeWave is hitting the economy that is not yet fully recognized by Wall Street?

The Blinding Flash of the Indefinite Obvious: What new secular ChangeWave has emerged, that is so powerful that it will continue to grow much faster than the overall economy? So fast that you can't ignore the opportunity?

My Big Investment Idea: In the context of all the no-brainer secular growth assumptions in the New Economy, and in the context of *all* of the secular economic growth engines in the economy, I judge the _____ sector, and the _____, its subsector, to be one of *the* prime beneficiaries of the _____ no-brainer secular growth assumption.

The SuperSpace Payoff Stock: Based on these assumptions, I believe that _____ is *the* company best positioned to capitalize on this significant, irreversible growth trend and thus is more likely than not to be rewarded by Wall Street with a rapidly appreciating stock versus other companies and opportunities that I could be investing my hard-earned money in.

Big Investment Idea: This investment is a _____ play on the _____ SuperSpace within the _____ SuperSector. My one-year price target for the stock(s) is $_____.

Primary ChangeQuake: The core enabling capability the company leverages.

Contributing Aftershock(s): Recent new capabilities that contribute to the KVP.

The Buyer and the Addressed Market Opportunity: Who buys this solution and how big (in dollars) is the addressed market?

Killer Value Proposition: What problem does this service/product solve, and in what proprietary order-of-magnitude-improved way does the company solve it?

52-week High/52-week Low: _____

50-Day MA, 200-Day MA: These are the 50-day and 200-day moving price averages. You need to know these numbers because they represent the two most critical price support levels for investors who are seeking to hold their investments to sell for capital gains (i.e., for at least one year and a day). For emerging SuperSpaces and E.G.O.D. stocks, I try to make sure I'm buying the stock above its 50-day moving average because buying an E.G.O.D. stock that is technically strong increases the odds of your success to your play.

Float: Float refers to the number of shares and percentage of the total issued stock that is in the hands of the public and not in the restricted hands of employees and executives of the company. The importance of stock float is the law of supply and demand. When you have correctly identified a SuperSpace about to get hit with a stream of money, you want to own companies whose stock is in short supply. In virtually all cases (QUALCOMM being the lone exception), the best performing E.G.O.D. stocks for us over the past four years have been ones with less than 8 million share floats—and in fact most of our big winners had floats of less than 5 million shares.

All things being equal, if I'm trying to decide between companies within a SuperSpace, the tie breaker many times is the one with a significantly lower float. Agile Software (AGIL) comes to mind: until Agile sold a secondary round of stock in late December 1999, it had roughly 3 million shares in float. This created panic-buying days where the stock moved from $15 to $40 in a day, because everybody "had" to own a leader in the e-supply chain SuperSpace. They had to buy AGIL. When there is more demand than supply in anything that has a price tag, the price moves up until the demand is satisfied.

Once the stock has graduated to game-over dominator status, then float becomes much less of an issue. In fact, large-cap stocks actually need a large float to maintain their value. Institutional investors require their large-cap holdings to trade enough stock every day for them to sell 100,000 shares in a day and not bring down the supply/demand ratio—which sinks the stock price.

TTM Sales Growth and TTM Earnings Growth: Trailing twelve-month (TTM) sales and earning growth tell you how fast the top line of your WaveRider is growing. In E.G.O.D. aggressive growth investing, these numbers must be eight to ten times the average growth of the S&P 500 stocks at minimum, or you don't have a growth stock. Most of our E.G.O.D. stocks grew their TTM revenue in excess of 100 percent.

Relative Price/Earnings/Group Strength: These numbers are available in *Investor's Business Daily*. As I've said before, I would not invest significant money in aggressive growth stocks without a subscription to *IBD*—it's the bible of the institutional aggressive growth managers.

Relative Price Strength measures your WaveRider company's upward stock price momentum against the entire market as a whole. The higher the number, the higher the company's recent stock price momentum is ranked against the market as a whole. In E.G.O.D. stock picking, you want your stock to be rated at least at the 70th percentile. This indicates that some people are buying it, but it has not been totally discovered yet. When an E.G.O.D. is ranked 90 or higher, you can bet the momentum buyers are already buying. This means the stock will do great while the SuperSpace is hot. But if it misses its projected sales numbers in even one quarter, the stock will get hammered as the "momo" (or momentum money) sells first and asks questions later.

Relative Earnings Strength measures your WaveRider company's earnings against the entire market. The higher the number, the better the company's earnings growth ranked against the market as a whole. This number is not vital to emerging sector stock picking but is crucial for emerged SuperSpaces and their game-over dominant player. In fact, there is an interesting correlation for emerging SuperSpace companies and very low relative earnings strength ratings: the right stock in the best space with a single-digit relative earnings strength number very often performs brilliantly. I can't tell you how many times this is true. Go figure.

Relative Group Strength measures the strength of the stocks broadly associated with your SuperSector against the entire market. The higher the number, the higher the industrial group's price momentum is ranked against the market as a whole. Being mindful of relative group strength keeps you out of doggy sectors. Remember that up to half of a stock's movement is due to the interest in the business sector in which it is categorized.

ChangeWave Strategic Fundamentals

Monster ChangeWave(s): If your WaveRider stock is not a direct beneficiary of one of the free world's four Monster ChangeWaves, you're not ChangeWave Investing, pal—you're freelancing.

SuperSector: Which top 10 percent CAGR sector is your stock related to?

Market Today/2003: These numbers are available from one or more of the market research organizations operating within the New Economy (Forrester, Jupiter Communications, IDG (International Data Group, etc.). The consensus of these firms for most sectors and spaces within the New Economy are available for free to registered users of *Change-Wave.com*. Many times, a simple Internet search on the sector or space name will bring you a wealth of analyst projections. But the kicker here is if there are no analyst projections about your selected SuperSector or SuperSpace, then you don't have one. If your sector or space is not on the radar of market analysts yet, you are too early.

CAGR Percent: This number is simply the total projected sector annual sales for the next two years minus total projected Year 1 sales divided by total Year 1 sales.

SuperSpace Fundamentals

Name of SuperSpace: The name of the sector space in which your emerging game-over dominator or game-over dominator WaveRider company exists.

SuperSpace Type: What type SuperSpace is this? A mission critical common-thread enabler (providing enabling component or infrastructure within multiple SuperSectors); strategic SuperSector enabler (sector-specific component or infrastructure); or direct-to-consumer?

SuperSpace Ranking: At *ChangeWave.com*, we rank the projected three-year market growth of most market spaces within the New Economy relative to the projected three-year growth rate of the aggregate market spaces. If you are working on a Big Investment Idea and you don't find your Super-Space listed at *ChangeWave.com*, e-mail us at *research@ ChangeWave.com*, and we'll do our best to find the data and post it. Obviously, ChangeWave Investing protocol expects you to stay in spaces in the top 10 percent growth rate relative to the New Economy spaces as a whole. Most of our winning E.G.O.D. stocks rank in the top 5 percent.

Market Today/2003: This is the percentage cumulative annual growth rate of the potential universe of buyers for the product/service in the SuperSpace, usually estimated by research houses and the companies within the space in their SEC filings or marketing web sites.

WaveRider Intellectual Property Category: What kind of intellectual property play is this company? Here are some examples: (1) enabling technology standard owner; (2) dominant mission critical common-thread enabler; (3) killer mass-market business model owner (think Dell or AOL); (4) proprietary killer application enhancement technology (i.e., a proprietary technology that enhances an already emerged killer application in the New Economy. Tumbleweed Communication's bid to become the standard for turning e-mail—the killer app of the Internet—into registered private mail is an example).

The Corporate WaveRating

I use the Wave scale to rate companies in 11 categories. A high score (4 to 5 Waves) in each category is necessary for E.G.O.D. and G.O.D. companies to execute their business model and to plan well enough to become the game-over dominators of their SuperSpaces.

> 5 Waves = 9 points. Excellent; as good as it gets.
> 4 Waves = 7 points. Very good, but not among the
> best you've ever seen.
> 3 Waves = 5 points. Nothing special; average.
> 2 Waves = 3 points. Lacking; below par.
> 1 Wave = 1 point. Worthless.

1. **Intellectual Property (IP) Rating:** We give 5 Waves (9 points) to companies with intellectual property that is patented, high leverage, high gross margin, mission critical common-thread enabling information technology. If a company has the intellectual property that has become the de facto industry standard that addresses huge potential markets or has the potential for ubiquity within the one or more of the Monster ChangeWaves of the economy, that's sure worth a 9 (think PC operating systems or QUALCOMM's CDMA patents).
2. **Corporate Vision Rating:** How big and how innovative is the company's strategy for the future? Great corporate visions are definitions of the

business in terms that other competitors don't use. I invariably find that the best performing companies in our portfolio define their business in completely different terms and ideas than the other companies in their field.

3. **CEO Maverick Rating:** Revolutions are led by nonlinear revolutionaries, not incremental improvers. How does the CEO rate as a rebel?

4. **COO Execution Rating:** A great vision without superb execution of the business plan is a tragedy for the company and its investors. How well does the company execute its business model on the field of battle?

5. **CFO Earnings Management Rating:** Wall Street hates surprises. The CFO's job is to manage the company's top and bottom line and Wall Street at the same time. You get a Wave for every two quarters the company has met or beat growth estimates on the top and bottom line.

6. **Market-Share Position Rating:** Number one gets 9 points. Number two gets 7 points. Everyone else gets 1.

7. **Corporate Culture Rating:** Nothing is more important to executing your business plan in a knowledge-based company than the quality of the corporate atmosphere and the strength of its culture. Great things come from people who want to make a difference and feel like they are allowed to do so. A "Top 100 Places to Work" rating, a below-industry-average turnover rating, or a high score from the ChangeWave Alliance rating gets you 5 Waves. Close to that bar gets you 4 Waves. This is the toughest asset to rate without having direct experience with the company, but it is too important to ignore. Use the CWA rating if there is one.

8. **Sales Team/Sales Power Rating:** How strong is the sales team? Virtually all game-over dominators

have the strongest sales force in their field. Coincidence? I think not.

9. **Strategic Alliances/Ecosystem Rating:** If you want to eat what the big dogs eat, you have to run with the pack. What connections to other game-over dominators has the company developed? What is the degree of influence on other companies in the space, and how deep are the relationships they maintain? An investment from a company at the top of the New Economy food chain like Intel, Cisco, or Microsoft is worth 2.5 points.

10. **Killer Value Proposition Rating:** How far ahead or locked-in is the company's value proposition to its customers versus competitive offerings? This rating must include up to 3 Waves for the uniqueness of the value proposition (i.e., how many others are doing essentially the same thing?) and up to 3 Waves for the degree of gap between competitors (measured in years or patent protection).

11. **Wall Street/Media Sponsorship Rating:** Who is "pounding the table" on the SuperSpace, and who is pounding the table on the company? Stocks will forever be sold not bought. The difference today is that stocks are sold by the financial, business, and New Economy media, the company's brand image, and Wall Street "sell side" analysts. Emerging E.G.O.D. companies in emerging SuperSpaces by definition have little Wall Street coverage but need to have sufficient news flow to feed the adrenaline of short-term investors. E.G.O.D. stocks must average at least four significant news releases (contract wins, alliance wins, design wins, etc.) per month for a 5 Wave rating.

Total Wave Rating Score: _____

Addressed Market Opportunity Index (AMO Index):
Part of our screening process in ChangeWave Investing is to evaluate the size of the market opportunity a company or space addresses relative to other fast-growing SuperSpaces. All things being equal, when choosing between two Super-Spaces growing at similar secular growth rates, our research indicates it's more profitable to invest in the SuperSpace addressing a significantly larger market opportunity. We analyze the size of the market opportunities addressed by the New Economy SuperSpaces at *ChangeWave.com* and establish an arithmetic average. The average market opportunity addressed becomes 1.00 on our AMO index. An AMO index of 2.00 means the market opportunity addressed by the SuperSpace is twice the New Economy average. The higher the AMO, the higher the eventual market valuation of that SuperSpace's eventual game-over dominator.

Average Gross Profit Margin: We use this screen to eliminate companies that don't have a scalable business. By "scalable" I mean that the costs to actually produce the service or product of a New Economy company should be relatively fixed so that when volume hits critical mass, gross profit margins (sales price minus cost of goods sold) stay high or go higher. One reason we have not bought any B2Me-commerce or web professional services companies other than Amazon.com is this scale issue. A company with a gross margin less than 50 percent does not make it on our team. Our usual cut-off is 70 percent or higher—and many of our WaveRider companies earn 80 percent gross margins.

A) Space Growth Rating: _____
B) Wave Rating: _____
C) Avg. IBD (*Investor's Business Daily*) Score: _____
  (Relative Strength (RS) plus Earnings per Share (EPS), divided by 2.)
Total WaveRider Draft Score (A+B+C): _____

Technical Fundamentals: _____
Average Volume: _____
Today's Volume: _____

1. **Speculative Buy Price:** (above 50-day average but 50% below 52-week high) $ _____
2. **Break-Out Buy Price:** (less than 5% of 52-week high on higher than average volume) $ _____
3. **Quick Cut Sell Price:** (8–10% below buy price) $ _____
4. **Secondary Upgrade Price:** $ _____ by _____ (20% up move within 4 to 6 weeks of purchase)
5. **Double-Up Price:** $ _____ by _____ (break-through of 52-week high on higher volume or 20% higher move from secondary upgrade price)

We rate each company in our universe on key business characteristics from direct research we've performed and from direct subjective analysis feedback we solicit from Change-Wave Alliance members. Once again, we post these ratings on *ChangeWave.com* for all to view and use for free.

If you want to participate in the ratings or get a company you are interested in rated by one of our Industrial Intelligence Panels, why not apply to join the ChangeWave Alliance and help us all out? Alternatively, you can e-mail *research@Change-Wave.com* and ask when a company you are interested in is scheduled to be rated.

If you can't award points in but a few categories about a company, it's a good indication that you need to go to Change-Wave Alliance and find more about any or all of the following criteria before you put hard-earned money into its stock.

WaveRider Draft Worksheet Case Study

Every successful investment analysis strategy system has a few stock recommendations that are emblematic of the strategy.

One of our big winners of the last three years that embodies everything within the ChangeWave Investing protocol is QUALCOMM. We are proud of the advice and proud of the way we owned it.

But perhaps a better case study of the ChangeWave Investing protocol and program in action is a recommendation we made last May that, up until recently, only a very few people knew about.

The company is named MicroStrategy. We recommended the stock at $21 on May 15, 1999 and it closed at $300 (now split 2-for-1) on January 25, 2000.

In many ways we are prouder of this research and recommendation because unlike QUALCOMM, Wall Street had hardly heard of MSTR and barely covered its remarkable story. That we heard of the company at all, and saw the blinding flash of the soon-to-be-obvious where no one else had, speaks volumes about the strength of the ChangeWave Investing approach. Here's how we created our ChangeWave worksheet.

WaveRider Worksheet: MICROSTRATEGY

Company's Name: MicroStrategy
Stock Symbol: MSTR
The League and the Play: Emerging sector E.G.O.D. play on the intelligent e-commerce software SuperSpace
The Blinding Flash of the Not-Yet-Obvious: E-commerce is over. What businesses and people want is Me-commerce: Nordstrom service, K-Mart pricing, 7-11 ubiquity, and Domino's delivery. To do this, you need an e-business intelligence capability and platform: a huge (terrabyte-plus) relational database with real-time database mining software matched with real-time *device agnostic* (i.e., cell phone, e-mail, PDA, etc.) broadcast technology. MicroStrategy is the far and away leader of this pivotal solution to the Me-commerce desires of the public and of Global 5000 companies.

My Big Investment Idea: In the context of the emerging New Economy, and in the context of all of the secular economic growth engines in the economy, I judge the Enterprise Internet software sector, and the intelligent e-business infrastructure industry space within that sector, to be one of the prime beneficiaries of the B2Me and B2B e-commerce secular growth engine (the number 3 and number 1 most powerful secular growth engines in our economy for the foreseeable future).

The WaveRider Payoff Stock: Based on these assumptions, I believe that MicroStrategy Inc. is *the* company best positioned to capitalize on this significant, irreversible growth trend and thus is more likely than not to be rewarded by Wall Street with a rapidly appreciating stock versus other companies and opportunities in which I could be investing my hard-earned money.

Primary ChangeQuakes: TCP/IP and HTML global standards for Internet computing.

Contributing Aftershock(s): The new WAP global standard for wireless Internet data connectivity and browsing.

The Buyer: Business people and individuals who want to individually control, select, and arrange for the trustworthy delivery of personal or professional information that's important to their communication device of choice.

Addressed Market Opportunity: One billion wireless Internet phone owners and one billion Internet users by 2005.

Killer Value Proposition: The ability for businesses and consumers to get *any* information that they find most relevant to their lives in real-time via *any* datacom or telecom device the customer prefers. MSTR enables businesses to deliver the right info to the right person at the right time in the right way.

52-week High/52-week Low: $41–$14.25

50-Day MA: $21   **200-Day MA:** N/A at purchase

Float: 6 million shares. Management owns 70 percent-plus of total stock. Founder controls 58 percent.

TTM Sales Growth: 98%

TTM Earnings Growth: 105%

Relative Price/Earnings/Group Strength: 72/85/89

CHANGEWAVE STRATEGIC FUNDAMENTALS
SuperSector: Me-Commerce Software Sector
Market Today/2003: $300 million growing to $5 billion
CAGR %: 112%

SUPERSPACE FUNDAMENTALS
Name of SuperSpace: Intelligent Me-Commerce Infrastructure
SuperSpace Type: Common-thread enabler
SuperSpace Ranking: 96th percentile
Market Today/2003: $75 million to $500 million
CAGR%: 143%
WaveRider IP Category: Proprietary Killer Application Enhancer. Makes
e-mail, wireless Internet, and telephony much more valuable.

THE CORPORATE WAVERATING
1) **Intellectual Property (IP) Rating:** 5 Waves. Nobody close in terrabyte real-time database mining.
2) **Corporate Vision Rating:** 5 Waves. The big vision: enabling people to set up their own personal private databanks where anyone on earth can ensure that they will be contacted if something they really care about occurs.
3) **CEO Maverick Rating:** 5 Waves. Mike Saylor started the company out of MIT at age 24. He's now 34. Declared 5 years ago the company would become a $1 billion revenue firm before he hit 40.
4) **COO Execution Rating:** 4 Waves: Have not missed a quarter in last 6.
5) **CFO Earnings Management Rating:** 4 Waves. Ditto.
6) **Market Share Position Rating:** 5 Waves. #1 in primary biz space. #1 in new emerging biz space: personal data intelligence management.
7) **Corporate Culture Rating:** 5 Waves. Top 100 Places to work in America.
8) **Sales Team/Sales Power Rating:** 4 Waves. Adding coverage will get to 5.
9) **Strategic Alliances Rating:** 5 Waves. Adding 10 key alliances per quarter.
10) **Killer Value Proposition Rating:** 5 Waves. Turns my digital devices into insurance delivery devices—makes them potentially 100 times more valuable to me.
11) **Wall Street/Media Sponsorship Rating:** Wall Street 1 point—need much more coverage. Media 4.5 points.

Total Wave Rating Score: 79.5 (95 as of 1/10/00)
Average Growth Profit Margin: 81%
A) Space Growth Rating: 95
B) Wave Rating: 79.5
C) Avg. IBD (*Investor's Business Daily*) Score: 82
Total WaveRider Draft Score (297 perfect): 256

The average WaveRider E.G.O.D. stock's total draft score at purchase is 210. So MSTR looked to be a screaming buy. Boy was it!

THE VALUE CHAIN

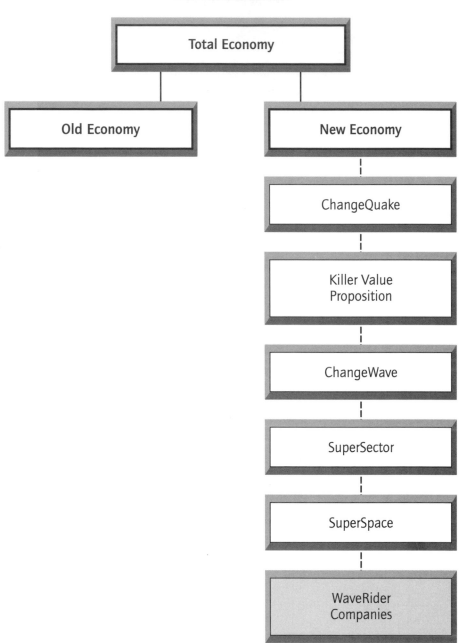

CHAPTER 18

Buying Monster Stocks

At the Right Time

We need to expand our ChangeWave mantra a little to make you into a great WaveRider stock-owner. "The right stock in the best space wins" expands to

> *The right stock in the best space at the right time wins.*

We've expanded the phrase to include the timing of your stock purchases. Just because a stock meets all your requirements and is a top 1 percent WaveRider company, *when* you buy and how quickly you sell can have as much to do with your success as what you buy.

When you make an aggressive growth investment, only four things can happen: you can make a large profit, make a small profit, take a small loss, or take a large loss. Only one of these is acceptable.

Our goal in stock picking is to have our winners up ten times more than our losers. To achieve this goal and by adhering to specific technical rules, we keep the odds of success on our side by being disciplined about buying and selling. Let's start with some rules for buying:

1. **Buy in an Uptrend:** Buy when the market is in an uptrend (as defined by the NASDAQ Composite Index moving above its 50-day average).
2. **Buy on a Reversal:** Buy stocks that have moved up at least 20 percent from a temporary downtrend (that test their 50-day moving average for E.G.O.D. stocks and 200-day for G.O.D. stocks).
3. **Double Up on the Movers:** Double up on stocks that have moved 20 percent higher in three to four weeks or less. According to William O'Neal & Company, publishers of the must-read investment newspaper *Investor's Business Daily* (and, I think, the finest market statistics outfit on Wall Street), of the 95 top performing small-cap stocks in 1996–1997 (companies under $5 billion market value), the ones that moved 20 percent or more in three weeks or less averaged 416 percent gains. Our stock-buying system tries to exploit this pattern by building positions up, and not chasing losing stocks down.
4. **Concentrate Your Picks:** Diversity, or holding 30 or 50 or 100 stocks in an aggressive growth portfolio, is the mother of mediocre results. The reality of investing in a bull market is that only a fraction of the thousands of stocks double or triple in price. In 1999, only 1.4 percent of the 8,000 stocks that started the year over $12 doubled in value. With your capital spread too thin, you boost the risk of losing out on a huge gain even if you do catch a Monster WaveRider stock. We try to add capital quickly to our winners and get rid of losers or slow

performers to concentrate our money in three to five of the biggest winners. You are playing the game well when you look at your biggest winners and see that you have the biggest amount of invested capital there. You are losing serious money if your biggest winners only have one-half or a full unit investment. Put more investment units in your biggest winners

5. **Buy on Up Volumes:** If a stock is going to continue moving higher, big mutual funds and hedge funds need to be buying it every day. This requires a great business in a great space—our ChangeWave Investing forte. But the way our Big Investment Ideas are proved valid is via human behavior—i.e., rising volume of shares being traded as our stock trends higher. No higher volume, no sustainably higher prices.

6. **Take Advantage of the Float:** Float is the amount of stock available for purchase. When lots of investors get excited about a stock and there are not many shares available, the limited supply helps drive the price up. Supply and demand works for stocks just like any other service or product.

The Float

When one of our WaveWatcher E.G.O.D. stocks have moved sharply up, virtually all have sold additional amounts of their stock in effect to strike while the proverbial iron is hot. This is fine. In fact, there are many institutional investors who are prohibited by the laws of their fund from buying the stock of a company with less than 5 million shares of available stock. So we don't sell when an E.G.O.D. floats a secondary offer. Since there is always a temporary imbalance or downturn the day of a secondary announcement, we use that day to add to our positions.

We have experienced many big moves on our companies with smaller than 5 million-share floats after the new stock is finally sold and added to the "float." These moves can be directly attributed to new institutional buyers now in the hunt.

The downside of a smaller than 5 million-share float is that volatility is dramatically enhanced with the level of private ownership. If only a small percentage of a company's stock is available in the public markets, you can bet the stock will fluctuate wildly. Agile Software (AGIL) comes to mind.

The issue is short-sellers—traders who have borrowed the stock and sold it in hopes they will be able to buy it back at a lower price and net the difference as profit. Well, when some big investor decides he *has* to own AGIL and starts bidding it up, guess what? There is not much stock to buy. So the stock-owners ask more for their shares; it starts to move up in $1 increments and then the short-selling panic sets in. You see, the short-sellers' profits are washing away as the stock moves up, and worse, to unwind their position they have to go into the open market and buy fast-moving stock to replace the shares they sold short. This creates panic buying or what is called a "melt-up"—the opposite of a meltdown.

The reverse happens when AGIL peaks. Now there are no short-sellers in the stock—this is not a good thing. When a big institution or momentum investor wants to unload a big chunk of stock, the way they attract buyers is to offer stock at lower price—i.e., put their inventory on sale. This action puts the buy/sell demand temporarily out of balance. And, with no short-sellers in the stock to buy stock on the way down to profit from their correct timing call, the stock hits an air pocket and can drop 10 to 20 percent in a day sometimes.

The point? Don't get shaken out of your emerging game-over dominator stocks by volatility once you have a big enough profit to absorb 5 to 10 percent swings. A good rule of thumb is let your E.G.O.D stocks bounce off their 10-week (50-day) moving averages. Look for less than 5 to 6 million-share floats for your E.G.O.D. companies in SuperSpaces (you can get the float off of *ChangeWave.com* or *Yahoo.com*). It's a great tell about the upward potential and volatility of a WaveRider stock.

Technical Aspects

Why worry about the "technical" aspect of aggressive growth investing?

First, great growth stocks move sideways or lower as they move ultimately higher. Without these sideways up-and-down periods of choppiness, called basing or consolidation, we'd never get rid of the short-term traders and low-conviction stockholders.

Second, successful aggressive growth investing is a game of higher high prices and higher low prices. The game is won when your stocks move to higher highs than their previous highest price and stop their descents at higher lows. Your entry price point counts.

We also look for "highly convicted" stockholders. We want to own stocks that current owners don't want to sell and that nonstockholders want to buy. These basing periods separate the weak from the strong stockholders and are vital to long-term 1,000 to 2,000 percent moves.

Ideally, we want to buy our WaveRider stocks as they are moving out of one of these bases. All great ChangeWave stocks pause from time to time for profit-taking to occur from short-term holders or institutional investors who have to trim their positions to maintain their "investment style" or holding concentration integrity. On any given day there are a dozen reasons why a big institution has to sell stock in your WaveRider that have nothing to do with the stock at all. So don't worry. When the selling imbalance is resolved, these stocks resume their uptrend. We find this new leg of growth is the most opportune time to buy.

Mark Minervini and his computers at Quantech Research Group have researched the biggest gaining stocks of the last 50 years (excluding penny stocks under $5) and the results have been validated by ChangeWave Research since 1995. To wit:

- Virtually all of the biggest winning stocks started their big moves above their 200-day moving average.
- 96 percent made their move near their 50-day moving average.
- 96 percent of those moves came after a general market correction.
- Virtually all the winners were new companies that had gone public within the last five years and had less than 10 million shares outstanding before their big moves.

We keep this historical context in mind as we scout and draft our WaveRiders.

Building Your Portfolio

I like to think of building portfolios like building a baseball club. The similarities are pretty striking.

I consider a stock I've bought to be one of the following:

- **A Minor Leaguer:** This is the stock's trial period. If it performs according to my Big Investment Idea, it stays and gets more money. If it does not, and drops 8 to 10 percent plus an extra 1 percent from there, the stock is cut from the team. I start an investment in a minor league stock with half an investment unit, or around $5,000 if $10,000 is the investment unit.
- **A Major Leaguer:** This is a minor league stock that has moved 20 percent or more in less than four to six weeks (180 days for a game-over dominator stock). Once the stock has made that move, I add the other half-unit. The idea is to load up on a fast moving stock before it makes too big a move. There is nothing worse in aggressive growth investing than to

open your portfolio to find your smallest actual investment in one of your monster growth stocks.

- **An All-Star:** This is a stock that has either made the 20 percent move in three weeks or less or has moved another 20 percent from its major league upgrade in less than a second three-week period. With All-Star stocks I double up my investment and overweight the stock vis-à-vis my other portfolio weightings.

Recommended Investment Game Plan

There are three things to consider when developing a plan for your New Economy investment dollars: (1) risk and reward, (2) the size of your investment unit in dollars, and (3) the allocation of dollars among types of stocks (players).

Risk and Reward

In chapter 16 we introduced the concept of three major sector groupings (leagues) according to their risk and potential growth. You probably remember the emerging, emerged, and classic growth groupings and each of their risk and reward profiles. When you decide your allocation among the leagues you may choose to place some of your investment dollars in each league or you may decide on only one or two leagues depending on your risk tolerance.

Investment Unit

After you decide how much money you want to invest in New Economy stocks you divide that number by the number of leagues you decided to invest in. If your New Economy investment dollars total $100,000 and you have decided to invest equally in all three leagues, you would be investing about $33,000 in each league. We suggest that you buy eight to ten stocks in each league you invest in. So, $33,000 divided by 10 stocks would equal an investment unit of $3,300 or a half unit of $1,650.

If you don't have $100,000 to put in New Economy stocks, don't worry. The old days of being penalized for odd-lot trades (less than 100 shares) are over. You can buy 50 shares or 10 shares online now for the same rate. The important thing is that you get started, however large or small the amount.

Stock Type

Earlier in this chapter I discussed the three types of players or stocks (Major Leaguer, Minor Leaguer, or All-Star) to have in your portfolio. After you have determined your allocation among the leagues and investment unit you're ready to decide what kind of players you want to draft (buy). You may already have some players on your investment team (stocks you purchased previously), so that needs to be part of your consideration. And, you need to consider what type of players you want in each league you've decided to invest in. The type of players may vary from league to league.

Here is my plan for the allocation among players:

- 50 percent of my money in my All-Star WaveRider stocks
- 20 percent of my money in Major League WaveRider stocks
- 20 percent of my money in Minor League prospects
- 10 percent cash

Unless you are comfortable with buying stocks with borrowed money (on margin with a loan from your broker), having a little cash around for a quick moving opportunity has always paid off for me.

This discipline forces you to make hard decisions on your minor and major league stocks. Where do you want most of your original investment capital? In a monster WaveRider Stock, up 1,500 percent, or a Major League WaveRider stock stuck at a 60 percent gain over the same time period?

Before I draft, I wait patiently for a stock to complete its basing period and look to strike when the stock hits its break-out point. You find the break-out point when the stock nears its 52-week high and then sells off a bit on 30 to 50 percent less trading volume. This is your signal—no one wants to sell the stock!

How do you know? Because there was 30 to 50 percent less stock available for sale that day. So the only people who sold stock were the weaklings or low-conviction owners still in the stock. Start your draft in an uptrending market.

The key to drafting your stocks is to get a daily report that shows you

- A chart of the last 12 months with 50-day and 200-day moving averages overlaid.
- The average volume of trading over the past 60 and 120 days.
- The volume traded for the day with the high and low prices.
- The 52-week high and low prices.

This data is available at many investment sites, including *finance.Yahoo.com* and *ChangeWave.com* for free. *finance.Yahoo.com* is a great place to find a table that arrays the trading volume of your WaveRider prospects (we hope to get this functionality to *ChangeWave.com*, too).

When you finish developing your plan you're ready to start drafting New Economy stocks and enjoying their monster growth. Use the WaveRider Buy/Sell Worksheet (see the end of this chapter) to consolidate your plans on one page.

New Economy Stocks Are Seasonal

Sy Harding, an investment analyst who has studied seasonality for years, has come up with pretty convincing evidence that most of the market gains—especially for New Economy companies—occur between November and May. His analysis is simple: this is when all of us get the most cash from bonuses and other compensation. I am most aggressive in drafting new stocks and moving them up between November and May. New studies released by Ibbotson Associates in the *New York Times* on February 25, 2000, detail how small-capitalization (under $1 billion) stocks' average annualized returns are 18.2 percentage points higher between November and April than between May and October. I try to build up cash and buying power in the summer.

Because of the propensity of the market to move up from the last trading day of each month through the fourth trading day of the following month, you could get even finer-tuned if you wish.

My advice? Buy your stocks during uptrends of the NASDAQ Composite when it is above 50-day moving average, and don't try to guess a bottom during a correction down. When the average has moved 20 percent off its most recent low and resumed an upward trend line, that's the all-clear sign.

Whatever you do, honor the 50-day and 200-day moving average "collar" around your Major League and All-Star WaveRider stocks. Don't mess with them during any market correction or basing period unless you need the money to double up a new All-Star stock. Sometimes to get to a meaningful amount of money in your best Big Investment Ideas, you have to cannibalize your team. That's how the game is played.

You have to decide how committed you are to your Big Investment Ideas.

WAVERIDER BUY/SELL WORKSHEET

New Minor League Stocks to Draft	Existing Minor League Stocks to Cut (Sell)

Existing Stocks to Add Second 1/2 Investment Unit	Existing Stocks to Double-Up to All-Star Team

INSTANT REPLAY: HIGHLIGHTS OF PART III

- ChangeQuakes can spawn Killer Value Propositions which create rapid, massive secular transitions or ChangeWaves.

- Killer Value Propositions offer new order-of-magnitude improvements in the status quo by giving customers a better, richer emotional payoff.

- There are currently four trillion-dollar ChangeWaves sweeping across the U.S. economy with more on the way.

- WaveMapping shows the value chain of enabling components or sectors and identifies the sectors, spaces, and companies that can benefit from the ChangeWaves.

- A SuperSpace holds an enabling position in the value chain, directly provides a Killer Value Proposition to multibillion dollar markets, and is growing at eight to ten times the overall economy.

- Stocks with the greatest potential are pure plays in emerging or emerged sectors and are usually mission critical common-thread enablers.

- Doing homework with the WaveRider Worksheet will make and save you money.

- Charts offer the basic supply and demand facts about a stock. Volume is not an opinion—it's where the rubber meets the road.

- ChangeWave Investing helps you buy the right stock in the best space at the right time.

PART IV

PROTECTING THE LEAD: OWNING YOUR WAVERIDER STOCKS

CHAPTER 19

Selling the Losers, Letting the Winners Ride

Milk the Cows, Shoot the Dogs

Physics teaches us that an object set in motion tends to stay in motion until stopped by an outside force. According to a recent MIT study, high performing small-cap stocks over a six-month period tend to continue to outperform the market in the subsequent six to twelve months, while losers continue to lose ground. So we adhere to a strict rule of milking the cash cows and quickly putting the loser "dog" stocks out of their misery at maximum losses of 8 to 10 percent. This discipline adds value to the next rule.

Give the Winners Room

Studies have shown that most great growth stocks spend 33 percent of their time going up or down and 66 percent going sideways. So we have to give our winners room to win. We do this by watching the 50-day and 200-day price-moving averages of our stocks and not reacting to day-to-day swings.

Great tech investor Alberto Vilar once said: "If three of us go to college together and I make A's, you make B's and the other guy makes C's, we all pass. Not true in technology investing. Technology stocks get A's or they flunk. Now, all I need in a 20 stock portfolio (to seriously outperform the market averages) is three of 20 that are going to become 10-baggers (10x your original investment). It's weeding out the B-students that is the toughest."

Investing in emerging New Economy companies is much more like venture capital investing than traditional stock market investing because of the valuation paradox we've talked about. Venture capitalists make their big money from only a few of their stocks—but with a few stocks up 20,000 to 40,000 percent, even 100,000 percent, you only need a few.

The real strategy behind picking monster stocks is to let emerging game-over dominator companies grow into game-over dominator stocks—and hang on for the ride. I can't tell you how many times QUALCOMM sank to its 200-day moving average but recovered to new highs. The same is true for all our other monster winners.

If nothing dramatic has changed in the SuperSpace ranking, the market opportunity addressed, or the strategic advantage your WaveRider is leveraging into market share or profit share leadership, keep your finger away from the mouse. Because the only thing worse than not ever owning a life-altering, monster growth stock is to have owned one and sold it about 10,000 points too soon.

Selling Rules

Everyone says the hardest part of investing is knowing when to sell. Here are some rules to help:

1. **For the G.O.D.s—Sell on the 200-Day Break:**
   Never sell game-over dominator stocks (our large and super-large-cap companies) until they break

their 200-day moving average and don't bounce back quickly, and their relative strength (as measured by *Investor's Business Daily*) drops below 70.

2. **For the E.G.O.D.s—Sell on the 50-Day Break:** Never sell emerging game-over dominator stocks (our small to mid-cap companies) until they break their 50-day moving average and don't bounce back quickly, and their relative strength (as measured by *Investor's Business Daily*) drops below 70.

3. **Sell When You Have a Better Idea:** When your research uncovers a new idea that is more attractive than your lowest performing stock, sell the low performer and buy your new Big Investment Idea.

4. **Sell on 8 to 10 percent Drop in Up Market:** Sell a Minor Leaguer on an 8 to 10 percent drop in an otherwise positive market (as measured by the NASDAQ 100 Index). Stay with your Minor Leaguer if you bought at its break-out point and it reverses to its 50-day average. But if it fails to return on higher volume, adios amigo.

5. **Sit Tight in a ChangeStorm:** When the market is hit by a ChangeStorm (10 percent or more overall correction), sit tight and don't sell a thing unless you have to. If you do have to sell something, sell your worst performers and reinvest in your best performers when they cross back over their 200-day or 50-day moving average.

Never Cheap

Every New Economy stock I have ever owned that was any good never looked cheap and always got ahead of traditional "fundamental" measures of value. Every one. They never were cheap, but when the institutions came to the blinding flash of the now obvious and "had to own the space and its leaders," the stocks always exploded in value.

Odds on Your Side

Remember that in the ChangeWave Investing protocol, you are doing more strategic thinking and analysis than literally 99 percent of the rest of Main Street investors—and many of the pros.

The SuperSpaces and Big Investment Ideas you choose to play, and the WaveRider stocks you draft to profit from your analysis, will be fast movers up and down. Your research, and the research of the ChangeWave Alliance members who may have helped you construct and validate your Big Investment Idea, really do put the odds of success on your side. Your stocks have a far better chance of going up than those of other investors who have not completed their ChangeWave Investing research.

The ChangeWave buy/sell/hold system is analogous to going to the blackjack table in a casino. Based on our five-year 150 percent annual growth track record, you will win more "hands" than you lose. With the hands you gain (assuming your average investment is $10,000 a stock), your annual average win will be $15,000 per hand. And your average loss, using our selling rules (sell on 10 percent drops), will be $1,000 per hand per year.

This is what I mean by putting the odds in your favor.

Breaking the Rules

The patterns we now see in our E.G.O.D. stocks give us some latitude in the 50-day moving average rule.

1. **Stay through a Secondary Stock Offering:** Give the stock some room if the company has sold a secondary or follow-on stock offering. Ten out of ten times this situation occurred in 1999, the stock recovered back over its 50-day average after the new stock was absorbed into the capital markets.
2. **Stay through the Acquisition:** Let the market absorb the news if the company acquires a competitor. Unless the acquisition is out of left field or

horribly overpriced, the market needs awhile to become familiar with most acquisitions.

3. **Stay through the Lock-up:** Check to make sure the stock you are looking to buy is not entering the end of its "lock-up period" (normally six months after the company has gone public). After the lock-up period, the insider owners are now free to sell their stock—they are no longer locked up. This period normally takes the stock down for a few weeks. But the right stock in the best space usually recovers.

4. **Wait out Software Companies:** Near the end of the quarter, wait out the software company's stock until the first few weeks of the new quarter. All software stocks lag at the end of a quarter, usually because the salespeople are using the quarter end as a deal closer with their prospects. Predictably, the first month of a new quarter is usually the best for these companies as they start to report their closed deals—and the earnings for completed deals start to hit the books.

More often than not, the right stock in the best space bounces off its 50-day or 200-day moving average. Because there are a hundred possible explanations for this phenomenon that defy analysis, I just accept the principle at face value.

Patience

WaveRider stocks go through consolidation or basing periods more often than they move up or down. As we've said, this is what great aggressive growth stocks do: they shake out the low-conviction owners and attract higher conviction owners as evidence of their emerging dominance becomes increasingly acute. Plus, you will have the roughly every-six-month ChangeStorm market meltdown. The game is won by your

WaveRider stocks hitting higher new highs and higher new lows.

If you've done your homework, but your once fast-moving stock is stalled, don't get trigger-happy. The day you decide to abandon your "nonmovers" may be the day before the big news flash and the 20-point upward parade to another 200-percent higher move.

The only time I sell my Major League stocks for non-movement is when I need the cash to double up my position in a new All-Star company. Then you are being a good portfolio manager. Trading up is concentrating your money in your best-performing stocks. This is how million-dollar aggressive portfolios are built.

CHAPTER 20

Staying in the Game

The final part of the ChangeWave Investing game is owning your stocks well. And the only way I have found to keep myself from over-reacting to the semiannual technology stock meltdown that occurs like clockwork is—you guessed it—a final metaphorical game.

The purpose of the game is to remind me of the unstoppable power of Monster ChangeWaves, SuperSectors, SuperSpaces, and E.G.O.D. and G.O.D. stocks when the whole investment world is temporarily coming apart at the seams.

Two Separate Things: A Company and Its Stock

Remember the game you played in elementary school called "Paper, Rock, Scissors"? The paper always covers the rock, the rock always smashes the scissors, and the scissors always cuts the paper. Each of the three elements could either vanquish or be vanquished by one of the other two. As you'll see, with ChangeWave Investing, the rules are far easier.

In any emerging industry, there will be times when you're a little unsure of your investment. After all, progress in anything involves setbacks. ChangeWave Investing is part of the real world and in the real world ChangeStorms occur.

To be a successful ChangeWave Investor you must be able to weather these ChangeStorms. Just as hurricane season comes every year, the high potential growth stocks that you select will be subject to periodic fluctuations. This part of investing will not change.

There will also be times when the entire market takes a downturn. At times the market is flat-out pessimistic. A company and its stock, however, are two separate things. The growth prospects and potential of a company bear little resemblance to the daily fluctuations of its stock price. The stock market is simply an indicator of people's moods and levels of optimism about the secular growth prospects of the stocks within the market.

Always recognize that the effects of discontinuous change, ChangeQuakes, and the emanating ChangeWaves are irreversible and will, over the longer run, overwhelm the daily blips and blops of the stock market.

ChangeStorms

A ChangeStorm is a temporary disruption in the stock market. It's a short-term bout of pessimism. It comes and goes. If you have the mental and emotional strength to ignore Change-Storms, then you're among a rare breed of investors.

The moment you buy an emerging game-over dominator stock, all around you, you'll be exposed to the pessimism of others. You'll hear reports that the stock market is taking a nosedive. You'll hear that the industry you invested in is experiencing problems. Yet, the vast majority of what you're exposed to merely represents the temporary.

The defining truth about ChangeWave Investing is Change-Waves represent fundamental change in how people will behave. If I have a true . . .

- Killer Value Proposition
- born from a genuine ChangeQuake that spawns
- a SuperSector ChangeWave and
- a SuperSpace ChangeWave . . .

then a temporary ChangeStorm can't overcome a Change-Wave. A ChangeWave will, except in the rarest of cases, always beat a ChangeStorm.

You've Got to Know When to Hold 'Em . . .

"I, Toby Smith, being of sound mind and body, acknowledge that every six months Laser-Pacific will experience a ChangeStorm because all companies in technology experience a ChangeStorm."

I write a note in my daily investing diary like this to myself with every stock I buy to remind myself that paper covers rock, rock crushes scissors, scissors cut paper, and ChangeWaves beat ChangeStorms. I don't mean to make light of the fear that market ChangeStorms strike in your heart. Again I use the kid's game because it helps me keep the big picture in perspective relative to the little picture. Use any analogy or mental picture that works for you.

Take a company in the emerging SuperSpace of digital television—Laser-Pacific—to make my point on Change-Storms. Laser-Pacific is an E.G.O.D. company in the business of transferring regular TV and movies to high-definition format. The company is a leading strategic enabler for the upcoming emerging HDTV SuperSpace.

Let's pretend we own Laser-Pacific. Due to investors' "temporary insanity," which has nothing to do with Laser-Pacific's emerging game-over dominator position, Laser-Pacific's stock will experience blips and blops of the overall stock market.

My reaction? These will not shake me. These will not prompt me to sell. These will not cause me to lose sleep at night. I expect them.

When my brow is sweaty, when my gut feels queasy, when I feel like barfing all over the upholstery, I will review my plan, and I will stay on course.

When the ChangeStorm hits, I go back to my analysis and my treasure map (if I had been able to draw one completely, and, with the help of *Changewave.com*, that's a lock) and remind myself of the soundness of this investment. I review my original hypothesis and why I bought it.

Next, I ask myself a fundamental question: Has anything changed?

If nothing has changed, then I sit tight and let the storm pass. The arena I'm playing in is one of higher highs and higher lows. So when Laser-Pacific stock temporarily retreats to a higher low, I know the odds are great that it will return to a higher high.

A Lifeboat for You

People are selling. People with great wisdom are saying that this downturn is for real, that this is the big one. Now you're in a high panic mode. You're susceptible to anything. You think to yourself, "I'm going to sell this and cut my losses." That's when you need to go to *ChangeWave.com*.

We'll listen to you.

We'll work with you.

We'll get you through this. A section on our web site will help you through your angst, fear, and panic attack. We've all been there.

Interactive support represents yet another fundamental difference between what people have done for decades in the face of ChangeStorms and how open source investing can make you a better investor. Isolated investors who panic and sell out often watch their great profits turn into mediocre profits.

What about Truly Ominous Storms?

Aren't there storms that overturn everything?

There are. A secular economic ChangeStorm—something that affects the entire society—could put a crimp in your plans. But they are few and far between. If a truck hits Alan Greenspan, some bozo takes over, and the Federal Reserve Bank starts making ill-advised wholesale policy shifts, then all bets are off. In that rare case, the storm does beat the wave.

No ChangeStorm will steer me away from a company that has the strategic technology in an emerging ChangeWave. No ChangeStorm is going to dissuade me from investing in a game-over dominator or an emerging game-over dominator company that

- owns the rights to some unalterable process or technology,
- has the dominant brand recognition in the market place,
- maintains patented or copyrighted intellectual property,
- has strategic alliances, or
- has any type of natural monopoly.

Staying Out of the Dark Zone

The worst emotional place you can be in as an investor is what I call the Dark Zone. Here you feel actual fear. You panic. You want to sell.

Yesterday, you were a ChangeWave believer. You were connected, getting online, visiting chat rooms, ordering over the Internet. You were taking advantage of all of these capabilities and more—profound ChangeWaves in how we communicate, gather information, and make purchasing decisions.

Yesterday, you believed the mantra: ChangeWaves beat ChangeStorms. You saw AOL grow from 5 million customers to 10 million, and then to 20 million.

Today, you believe in getting out of the market as quickly as you can.

Welcome to the Dark Zone.

If the entire market is headed down and pessimism runs amuck, it's not out of the ordinary for one or more of your best E.G.O.D. All-Star winning stocks to plummet by half. Sometimes you'll see this happen over a month or two months in a market correction.

When the whole market is on a downturn, it is in a MarketStorm. Think of this downturn as a big, big ChangeStorm. It is a complete but temporary change in the psychology of the investing herd.

The fundamentals of why you bought the game-over or emerging game-over dominator stock haven't changed, and thus a month or two-month-long MarketStorm should not dislodge you from your bold position. This is the tough part of the game.

Stocks that outperform the market 3-5-10 to 1 are the first stocks to get a big haircut when the whole world gets nervous and temporarily runs for the exits. You should expect the best growth stocks to correct 2.5 to 3.5 times the amount of the overall market correction in a MarketStorm. Remember, this oh-so-fun phenomenon occurs in the New Economy stocks about every six months. I call this exercise in nerves a regularly scheduled market meltdown.

And if you don't recognize the periodic, but temporary nature of a MarketStorm, it can suck you into a Dark Zone panic that you may regret for years.

Pre-experiencing a MarketStorm

Here's a quick way I've found to stay out of the Dark Zone—rehearse the situation before it strikes. I like the concept of "pre-experiencing" a situation before it really happens. So take a moment and pre-experience a good old, semiannual market meltdown.

Imagine you own a lot of real estate in Key West, Florida. There's a hurricane alert. You've taken all the precautions and decided to stay in your residence. The contractor has assured you that the structure can withstand winds of up to 275 mph—in other words, double the force of a strong hurricane. You rationally accept this fact.

Similarly, you also rationally accept the fact that the New Economy has happened. Another 10,000 people will be connected to the Internet today and tomorrow and every day for at least the next three years, unless of course there is a worldwide catastrophe. This is a low-probability event, but there is a remote possibility that it could happen.

Back to our hurricane. When the storm hits, you're inside your house. The winds are howling; you're mentally prepared for this. After a while, a portion of your roof rips off. In a flash, you find yourself in the Dark Zone. You've been spooked. You've read the owner's warranty to your house over and over again. However, when you read it previously, you read it with optimistic eyes.

This time, you rush to the drawer, grab the warranty, and read through it with your pessimistic eyes. Sure enough, some caveat in a subclause now catches your eye. Is it a loophole? Is it something the contractor hadn't considered? Is its interpretation ambiguous?

Back to investing. You own six emerging game-over dominator stocks, and four game-over dominator stocks. Your stocks are up 150 percent over the previous year. Things could hardly be better. Then a ChangeStorm starts to brew. Market reports say there's a gross over-evaluation. The dollar is getting a little higher. Or there's a hint of inflation.

Suddenly, the news turns bad—a MarketStorm or 10 percent-plus "correction" appears on the horizon. You hear about how the market is heading down. You read that the Internet bubble is going to burst. When any of these pessimism-inducing events occur, you must go back to the letter you wrote yourself at the outset and read it slowly and carefully. Why?

Waves Beat Storms

One night, you find yourself tossing and turning. You start thinking to yourself how you spent lots of the paper profits you've made on the stocks. You remember the down payment on your condo in Aspen . . . that little Jason is not so little anymore and will be going to college soon. The next morning you read the paper and come across some pessimistic report on the market, or worse, on the industry in which you have invested. Now, instead of the scary words deflecting off you, they begin to sink in. And you succumb. Your fear overcomes your logic. This is when it is absolutely essential that you remember this fundamental: Monster ChangeWaves always beat Market-Storms.

Waves beat Storms. Always.

The hurricane blows through. There's some damage, but everything is in tact. The sky is clearing. Things are going to be fine, until the next hurricane.

Repeat the above like a mantra—MonsterWaves beat MarketStorms, Waves beat Storms. Maybe not immediately, but you can count on it. Unless you have a compelling reason why you need to sell any of your investments—such as a family emergency—your job as an investor is to stay put. Review your original notes, the treasure maps, and read your underlying rationale for each investment . . . Why did you buy, why did it make sense, why this industry, why now? Thoroughly refamiliarize yourself with the soundness of your analysis. The wisdom of your decision to buy. Your decision to hold until your stocks reached some predetermined selling point. The magnitude of the ChangeQuake shift is still the same.

If the ChangeWaves are just as strong, if the game-over dominating company or emerging game-over dominator still holds a sustainable competitive advantage, then from an investment standpoint, don't do a thing. If nothing has changed, then hold on to the stock. It may drop so quickly in just a few days, you feel your stomach churn. I don't care if the stock goes down 20 percent, 30 percent, even 50 percent. That is the nature of investing in aggressive growth stocks.

You had the guts to buy. Now have the guts to stay.

Feel the Fear and Don't Succumb

If it helps, when you're in the Dark Zone, stop reading the newspaper. Turn off the TV. Don't get on the Internet and visit stock report sites. And, sure as heck, don't talk to people who you know will bring you down.

Paradoxically, the moment that you feel yourself slipping into the Dark Zone is the lowest trough of the storm. Not only are you feeling it; everyone else is too. Remember, human behavior has been in formation for thousands of years. En masse, human behavior is immutable. When people slip into the Dark Zone, they panic. They make irrational decisions. They sell off what would've been perfectly lucrative investments.

Come to *ChangeWave.com*, and we'll talk you through it. We maintain a MarketStorm Dark Zone discussion group every night during the regularly scheduled market meltdowns. There is even a "panic button" you can click to get to the discussion group. Being in communication with other ChangeWave investors is the best way I know to kick the Dark Zone.

CHAPTER 21

Postgame Commentary

The No-Brainer Investment Strategy

Now that you understand the ChangeWave Investing protocol, you get to know a little secret. ChangeWave Investing really just mimics the most pervasive and dominant investment style of our time—what I call "no-brainer" aggressive growth investing.

We use our concepts of ChangeQuakes, Killer Value Propositions, ChangeWaves, and our investing laws like the Rule of Disproportionate Return to help us establish what we think Wall Street's current and future "no-brainer" growth stories or secular growth assumptions are for the New Economy.

As you know, capital flows toward the most predictable, locked-in places of long-term, rapid growth. That's why no-brainer growth investing is the dominant strategy of our era: in the highly volatile, nonlinear, rapidly transforming world of the New Economy, human nature drives investors—both professional and amateur—to put their growth money *in the surest things they can find.*

And in today's world, the surest investment around is investing in the stocks which everyone believes are the primary beneficiaries feeding on the biggest "no-brainer" secular growth stories of the New Economy.

Since no-brainer growth investing is the style du jour, ChangeWave Investing models its components. Think of no-brainer growth investing as a series of simple questions (these may sound familiar):

1. **The No-Brainer Secular Growth Assumption Question:** What are the biggest, locked-in no-brainer growth stories of the New Economy?
2. **The No-Brainer Sector Beneficiary Question:** Which industries are the primary no-brainer beneficiaries from these no-brainer growth engines?
3. **The No-Brainer Company Beneficiary Question:** Which companies within these strategically advantaged industries are the no-brainer winning stocks?

No-brainer investing starts by establishing the world's biggest, most massive no-brainer secular growth *assumptions*— what you know as the blinding flashes of the obvious that we use to establish the four Monster ChangeWaves of the New Economy. Currently the most widely held no-brainer 2000–2005 secular growth assumptions on Wall Street include

- Internet traffic doubling every 100 days
- 300 to 500 million people on the Net (5 percent monthly growth)
- Virtually 100 percent of businesses and organizations adopting Net-based electronic business processing, marketing, and procurement
- 80 to 90 percent of the $2 trillion in Internet commerce to be conducted business-to-business

- 1 billion interconnected computers
- 1 billion wireless Internet-connected phones
- Data storage doubling every year

Now with these no-brainer macroeconomic secular growth assumptions in hand, go to question two: Which industries are the no-brainer primary beneficiaries from these no-brainer growth engines?

You know the no-brainer answer: the New Economy infrastructure and understructure enabling sectors. Why? Because you learned the world's prevailing no-brainer investment logic in our little parable in chapter 4—"in times of revolutionary change, buy the bullet makers, not the bullet users."

Which enabling infrastructure and understructure industries are the no-brainer winners? The industries with the fastest growing industrial sectors we call SuperSpaces—outgrowing 90 percent of all other industries in the economy. For example, take our first two no-brainer secular growth assumptions:

- Internet traffic doubling every 100 days
- 300 to 500 million people on the Net (5 percent monthly growth)

Who is the no-brainer sector beneficiary? The high-speed bandwidth sector.

What are the no-brainer bandwidth *infrastructure* Super-Spaces? Optical networking components.

What are the no-brainer bandwidth *understructure* Super-Spaces? Lasers, fiber optics, and communications chips that enable optical networking.

Which stocks are the no-brainer winners in these Super-Spaces? The emerging game-over dominators and game-over dominators, of course. In optical networking components, the game-over dominator is JDS Uniphase. In optical communications chips, the E.G.O.D. companies are PMC-Sierra and Applied Micro

Devices. Need proof of the dominance of no-brainer investing? Look up the one-year price charts of JDSU, PMCS, and AMDD.

Where the ChangeWave Investing research protocol really shines is helping you identify Wall Street's *soon-to-be* no-brainer secular growth assumptions—the fantastically profitable blinding flashes of the not-yet-obvious.

Applying our stock-picking protocol to capitalize on your soon-to-be no-brainer secular growth assumptions simply helps you play this game a few steps ahead of the crowd—therein lies our advantage.

It's just not any more complicated than that.

Congratulations!

You're done. Now my goal for you is to arrive at one of two conclusions. Either

A. the ChangeWave Investing track record is a fluke and not consistently repeatable; or
B. ChangeWave Investing looks attractive and repeatable—you're ready to get into the aggressive growth game with some of your investable cash.

We hope you pick B.

But no matter what your choice, I hope you've come to a few conclusions about what is indisputably new about the world you live in.

The World in 2005

Indisputably there is an ever-increasing rate of change in our world. Which of course means an ever-increasing rate of market opportunities. When you stop and ask yourself "How will the world be different by 2005?" it's a virtually certainty that

- The cost/speed of microprocessors will have dropped/improved by at least 1,000 percent.

- If available bandwidth is tripling every year (Gilder's Law) then we will have 15,000 percent more telecommunication bandwidth capacity than we do today.

- There will be in excess of one billion users of the Internet.

But those computations recognize only linear improvements in the now. If we've learned anything from the New Economy revolution it is to expect nonlinear change. We're most excited about new discontinuous ChangeQuakes, new resulting Killer Value Propositions, and the resulting highly profitable ChangeWaves just around the corner.

In the New Economy, what's also indisputable is when you connect the entire world together into one giant knowledge and information database, expecting the unexpected becomes the norm. You should be expecting nonlinear changes in everything you think is already impossibly fast or impossibly high.

More Change

When you free your mind of its Old Economy mentality boundaries, the possibilities and potential for your future is startling. What's truly staggering to me is the magnitude of ChangeWave investment opportunities that lie ahead if one is to assume that today's frame of reference for change is *understated*. Today we are extrapolating the future using the reality of today's technology. What if you were to smash that mental prison and imagine the next few years' technology?

Today University of California Berkley researchers have a design for a new kind of transistor that is *one-twentieth* the size of today's smallest transistors—and will lead to chip devices that will store 400 times as much data as today's densest microchips at vastly lower prices.

Molecular-scale electronics is coming, and it's coming fast. Microelectromechanical systems, or MEMs for short, have the potential to accelerate the power and speed of every part of the New Economy "understructure" by *one hundred orders* of magnitude. Labs today are testing optical switches that would cost 1/1000 of today's highest speed photonics and are capable of multiplying the speed of the Internet 10,000 percent. IPv6—the next Internet communication protocol—is on deck. With it you can connect everything to everything. Who knows what KVPs this new capability will bring?

The point? Let your mind be free, and watch the change that follows. In the words of my favorite "economist" Richard Pryor: "Who are you going to believe? Me or your own lyin' eyes?"

The Wrap-up

When it comes to the ChangeWave Investing model for New Economy stock picking, you now know that "the right stock in the best space at the right time wins" *really* means:

The *right* New Economy stock within

- an emerging SuperSpace that's a pure-play, 15 percent-plus market share owner
- an emerged SuperSpace that's the number one or number two pure-play emerging game-over dominator market share leader
- a classic growth SuperSpace that's the pure-play game-over dominator

and whose management team is Wave rated over 70 points by you or by a ChangeWave Alliance Industrial Intelligence Panel with a total Wave rating of over 200 points.

In the best New Economy *space*

- with a CAGR ranking in the top 10 percent (or less) compared to other New Economy spaces within its category
- addressing a market opportunity rating of 1.0 or higher
- with Monster ChangeWave lineage (i.e., directly related to a Monster ChangeWave)

- preferably a mission critical common-thread enabler

At the right *time*, or first purchased

- in an uptrending NASDAQ market (over NASDAQ's 200-day moving average)
- above its 50-day and 200-day moving averages
- aggressively—20 percent or more above its most recent higher low the day after the stock moves slightly (10 percent) lower on significantly less (40 to 50 percent) than average 60-day trading volume
- safely—after a breakout from its most recent high price after a 5 to 8 weeks' consolidation period on significantly (40 to 50 percent) higher volume

With the right *portfolio weighting*,

- half an investment unit for an initial position (a.k.a. Minor Leaguer)
- second half of unit added at 20 percent gain within 30 to 60 days of purchase (a.k.a. Major Leaguer)
- 100 percent additional if the stock hits another 20 percent gain within 30 to 60 days (a.k.a. an All-Star)

The goal is to have your biggest initial investments in your most appreciated stocks—that's the right portfolio weighting. Fifty percent of your cash in your All-Stars, 20 percent in your Major Leaguers, 20 percent in your Minor Leaguers, and 10 percent cash reserve (or margin).

The Payoff

Following this game plan puts your odds of earning a decades' worth of portfolio growth every one to two years squarely on your side.

Adding 50,000 to 100,000 research hours of ChangeWave Investing investment intelligence-gathering and analysis each year to your own investment program (via your participation in the ChangeWave Alliance or using *ChangeWave.com*'s research and investment tools) raises the odds of achieving your aggressive investing goals by many orders of magnitude.

You know the game now. You know how we play it. We look forward to playing it with you.

INSTANT REPLAY: HIGHLIGHTS OF PART IV

- Milk the cash cows and quickly sell the dogs.

- Monster ChangeWaves always beat the MarketStorms.

- "No-Brainer" aggressive growth investing provides answers to three simple questions:

    - What are the biggest, locked-in no-brainer growth stories of the New Economy?

    - Which industries are the primary no-brainer beneficiaries from these no-brainer growth engines?

    - Which companies within these strategically advantaged industries are the no-brainer winning stocks?

PART V

THE HOME TEAM

CHAPTER 22

The ChangeWave Alliance

The Secret Sauce

Nobody is saying that our 150 percent-plus annual performances are sustainable long-term. What we are saying is, that properly practiced, the ChangeWave Investing protocol combined with hundreds of thousands of research hours dedicated to intelligence-gathering and analysis by the ChangeWave Alliance's worldwide network puts the odds of outperforming the market as measured by the S&P 500 Index *substantially* on your side.

And in investing, gaining, and maintaining an investable edge over the general market—the "secret sauce"—is what separates consistently high performers from the rest of the pack. We think the secret sauce of the ChangeWave Investing protocol is obviously the dedicated, investable intelligence-gathering and analysis research hours within the open source investing platform.

It is my most fervent desire that we will refine the open source investing movement the way Red Hat jet-powered the Linux open source software movement. We hope the simplicity of our screening system through ChangeQuakes, KVPs, ChangeWaves, and WaveRiders—plus the emotional management techniques of ChangeWave Investing *combined with* the real-time ChangeWave Investing "help desk" and worldwide virtual community of New Economy professionals—will, by definition, create a revolution in how people go about buying growth stocks for their portfolios.

How ChangeWave Investing Can Best Work for You

Charles Schwab and Company conducted extensive research into the basic style or type of investors. They came up with three basic types:

1. **The Self-Directors:** These investors do their own research and analysis soup-to-nuts. Self-Directors are interested in quality research that helps them make up their own minds as to what to buy, sell, and hold. About 5 to 8 percent of the investing public.
2. **The Validators:** These investors have a very good idea about where they want to be investing, and a good idea about the companies that pay off their ideas. But the Validators (for a variety of reasons) are more comfortable getting third-party validation, feedback, and refinement to their ideas before plunking down hard-earned cash. About 30 to 40 percent of investors.
3. **The Offloaders:** These investors do not want to be involved in their investments. The Offloaders prefer someone else to invest their money so they can do other things. About 30 to 40 percent of investors.

If you've gotten this far in *ChangeWave Investing*, I'm gonna guess you are either a Self-Director or a Validator. Which is good because we can help both types become successful ChangeWave investors. Offloaders? Maybe one day we'll have a mutual fund for them.

Obviously our system works great for self-directed investors who spend a fair amount of time doing their own research—the investor hobbyist, if you will. It also works wonders for those lucky enough to be working in one of these "most favored" SuperSector or SuperSpace industries and who possess enough personal knowledge of the industry to scout out the "right companies" within the fortunate space. But what about those of us who don't work in one of the Wall Street's anointed "right spaces" and don't have ten or more hours a week to devote to stock research?

Two Options for Two Audiences

We offer two options. New Economy professionals (i.e., those employed in or professionally trained in information technology, sciences, or knowledge-based service industries/ professions) can apply to join the network of ChangeWave Investing practitioners we call WaveWatchers in the Change-Wave Alliance (CWA). And, we have another option for those who are not New Economy professionals. We will discuss that later in this chapter.

The ChangeWave Alliance Pitch

The CWA is in essence a co-op of credentialed, profiled ChangeWave Investing practitioners who spend their everyday professional lives working in the frontline of New Economy industries or professions. Just like in the open source software world, in return for free access to the end-results research of the community, CWA members contribute their eyes, ears, and brains to the community. CWA members in turn join one or more space-specific teams we call Industrial Intelligence Panels (IIPs).

The IIPs are organized around many of the emerged and emerging sectors within the New Economy. More IIPs are launched every month. The IIP teams are moderated by a *ChangeWave.com* staff member or IIP volunteer and have one purpose in life: within their sector, they seek to discover and validate investable opportunities as defined within the Change-Wave Investment research protocol.

Why Should You Invest Your Time in the CWA?

The easiest answer is to significantly improve the odds of your getting rich. Or if you're already rich, then getting substantially richer.

Here's the math behind that claim.

Years ago brilliant young technologist Bob Metcalfe was trying to sell a new networking technology he called Ethernet. He coined the term "Metcalfe's Law" to reflect the unique logic behind the power of a network. As Kevin Kelly describes this math in his seminal work *New Rules for the New Economy,* "Mathematics holds that the sum value of a network increases as a square of the number of members. In other words, as the number of nodes (connections) in a network increases arithmetically, the value of the network increases exponentially."

The Internet itself is perhaps the best example of this so-called "network effect." E-mail wasn't valuable to you until a critical mass of people you communicated with had it. Take the fax. When most people had one, yours became more valuable to you. Now when you buy a fax for $100, you don't just get a piece of equipment. You are buying access to an entire network of 20 million-plus machines. Each additional machine sold increases the value of your machine. In short, in a network, the more plentiful things become, the more valuable they become.

When you add to this calculus the many academic studies that find the more diverse a group is—the higher the quality of decision making, you start to get the logic behind the power of the ChangeWave Alliance.

In a nutshell, when *you* join the ChangeWave Alliance network, the network becomes more valuable to the existing participants. The next invitee who joins makes the network more valuable to you. And so on and so on. Every new credentialed, participating member increases the richness and reach of the entire network's intelligence-gathering and processing. Each new "node" in the CWA network raises the odds of the success for *all* members and subscribers receiving the end-results advice.

Every time we increase the richness and reach of our intelligence, we add another 100 or so investable intelligence-gathering and analysis research hours to our system. And every quality research hour we add to the system means we get closer to our next monster SuperSpace and monster WaveRider stock.

But what makes the network work in the context of discovering and communicating investable intelligence is its common focus, protocol, language, and peer-review improvement process.

The Power of Many, Focus of One

Whereas other networked investment communities have a group of many but the power of none, we have the power of many and the focus of one. Rather than being the tower of investment babble online or essentially an entertainment media, our ChangeWave investment alliance members identify ChangeWaves, help prepare SuperSector and SuperSpace maps, and help identify game-over and emerging game-over dominators—to the benefit of everyone in the alliance.

Our members are credentialed professionals within the New Economy. Therefore, auto mechanics, day-traders, and other laypersons who lack these credentials and expertise cannot make the same contribution and are not invited to participate at this level.

What we're trying to do is create the Mensa of open source investing. The power of the network is multiplied by an even greater number than Metcalfe's Law by adding high quality reach dispersed over hundreds of New Economy spaces. Limited to qualified members, our investment research improves in the same way that the Linux operating system and Apache software, other open-source systems, have been so successful. Qualified members send in improvements such that the system benefits from a continuous stream of investable intelligence that no hired staff could emulate.

50,000 Smart People Are Better than One

We project the network to grow to 50,000 credentialed members by year-end 2001. Think of the power of 50,000 people—and 500,000 research hours per year—relaying intelligence from all the current SuperSpaces and SuperSectors into one central intelligence-gathering and analyzing organization! Fifty thousand people who have studied, played with, toyed with, dabbled with, invested in, spoken about, written about, and researched investable opportunities in real-world situations all day long. You can't buy expertise like that. Wall Street can't buy a force like that.

The WaveWatcher Game

Each ChangeWave Alliance member becomes a member of one or more SuperSector and SuperSpace Industrial Intelligence Panels. We field these panels to get these best and brightest members all on the same page. The kick is their contributions get graded. No fooling. We learned this concept from the wildly successful open source portal *Slashdot.org*, which has turned peer-review critiques into a science. Our underlying rationale is that just because you've been invited to become an alliance member (membership is good for one year), that doesn't mean you get to stay in forever.

You have to continue to earn your keep. The membership fee for the CWA is nominal—we don't want your money; we want your brain. All of the other members of the ChangeWave investment community are counting on you. We all count on each other. That's why our community is so powerful and unprecedented.

Our WaveWatchers' intelligence submissions are graded for value, and if your contributions aren't graded "B" or higher by your professional peers at the end of the year, *hasta la vista*, baby. We don't need the biggest network—we want the smartest.

Why do so many New Economy professionals all over the world actively participate in such a potentially humiliating sport as the ChangeWave Investing game?

You could say it's greed. They know that the more people participate in the network, the greater their chances for catching the next QUALCOMM or AOL wave in their portfolio.

It's also for the recognition. Never underestimate the personal value of braggin' rights. At the end of each year, we award "the Green Hawaiian Shirt" and significant cash prizes to the WaveWatcher and SuperSpace panelists who submit the most profitable ChangeWaves, Aftershocks, or emerging game-over dominator or game-over dominator stocks.

The perks are pretty valuable, too. Members get fantastic firsthand intelligence on what's really going on in their industry—frontline competitive intelligence reports that are not available anywhere else in their industry. For many, just the value of this perk alone is worth their time contribution ten times over.

Most members find WaveWatching to be fun! It's fun to play the game—it's fun to reap the rewards—and it's fun to win.

There is also a fantastic emotional payoff: the feeling you get when you know a space or stock that you identified turned in a monster growth performance. The feeling is fantastic because you will get e-mail after e-mail from fellow members and advisory subscribers telling you that your Big Investment Idea changed their financial world. Every year there are Wave-Watchers who can now afford to send Jenny to Harvard because of what one member's ChangeWave or ChangeQuake field report meant to their portfolio. I can tell you from personal experience that pride and emotional payoff are just as sweet as opening up your portfolio statement and seeing a new "zero" added to your balance (Okay, almost as sweet).

Most CWA members are invited to participate in this open source investment research virtual community by members who are friends and business associates. Readers should note you can nominate yourself as well for the CWA at *ChangeWave.com*.

You may be thinking, "Okay, the alliance program sounds good, but I don't know if I want to be in it or not. Sounds like a lot of responsibility. I'm not sure if I have the time, and maybe I'm not even qualified in terms of my industry background. Can I still benefit from your program?" The answer is absolutely yes. You can take advantage of our investment intelligence just like those who are not eligible to join the alliance.

So, You're Not a New Economy Professional

We have another option for more information for those who do not qualify for CWA membership but desire to expand the richness and reach of their personal investment intelligence gathering. You may prefer to simply get to the end-results advice generated via the ChangeWave Alliance investable intelligence processing system. For you, as well as for New Economy professionals who don't want to join the alliance, we offer a subscription. The *New Economy Investing* newsletter is available for a very reasonable annual fee. I serve as the editor of the advisory service. The subscription is available at *ChangeWave.com*. It comes with a 100 percent money-back guarantee if at anytime you don't find the end-results advice worth the subscription cost.

Conclusion

Whether you are a do-it-yourselfer, a do-it-for-me investor, or somewhere in between, no one who chooses to use the ChangeWave Investing system should feel left out of the loop. I firmly believe that, should you choose to pursue your aggressive growth investing via the ChangeWave Investing method, you will vastly improve your investment results no matter how you choose to play the game.

APPENDICES

- **ChangeWave Investing Glossary**

- **Bibliography**

- **ChangeWave Investing Track Record**

ChangeWave Investing Glossary

Addressed Market Size Rating: An index of all the sectors and spaces identified and tracked at *ChangeWave.com*. The average addressed market size is 1.00 on the index. An addressed market size twice the average would be rated 2.00.

Big Investment Idea: An optimistic high-growth core investment thesis or projection about a company's stock within the New Economy. Assumes it will become and remain the most highly valued by Wall Street and Main Street investors.

Business Model: In the New Economy it means:
1. What does a company do?
2. How does a company uniquely do it?
3. In what way (ways) does the company get paid for doing it?
4. How much gross margin does the company earn per average unit sale?

The Blinding Flash of the Not-Yet-Obvious: The economic or strategic ChangeWave that research indicates is *going to become* highly investable.

The Blinding Flash of the Obvious: The economic or strategic ChangeWave that research indicates is going to *stay* highly investable for the foreseeable future.

Broadband InfoGenesis: The trillion-dollar shift from terrestrial narrow-band, separate voice-and-data connectivity to utility-grade understructure for the high-speed processing, storage, and delivery of digital, packet-based voice, data, audio, or video information transported down one pipe to anywhere, to any device, all over the world. As of January 15, 2000, one of the four Monster ChangeWaves.

Business-to-Business E-Commerce (B2B): The trillion-dollar shift from analog, client/server, and EDI-based commerce to electronic B2B Digital Direct Interchange within digital, Internet Protocol–based intelligent trading environments. As of January 15, 2000, one of the four Monster Change-Waves.

Business-to-Me-commerce (B2Me): The trillion-dollar shift from e-commerce to a second-generation "me-centric" intelligent and personalized commerce via *any* media: store, phone, browser, personal digital device, or Web. As of January 15, 2000, one of the four Monster ChangeWaves.

CAGR: Cumulative Annual Growth Rate.

ChangeQuake: The eruption of new, potentially transformational technological, regulatory, economic, or strategic capability. ChangeQuakes can spawn Killer Value Propositions (KVPs), which create rapid, massive secular transitions or ChangeWaves within marketplaces.

ChangeStorm: The clockwork-like, once every six months or so "market meltdown" of the technology sector in general, and the New Economy stocks in particular. Seasonal money flow and trading patterns make the May through October season particularly difficult for high growth, high P/E stocks like New Economy stocks. Once this period is passed, stocks (for a variety of economic and behavioral reasons) blossom between Halloween and the beginning of May.

ChangeWave: Shorthand for a rapidly growing, highly investable secular economic or strategic transition. Economic ChangeWaves include industrial spaces and companies that facilitate the secular transition. Strategic ChangeWaves occur at the company level when a shift in leadership or business strategy redefines the value proposition for the business or increases the addressed market by an order of magnitude. ChangeWaves are the basis for "no-brainer" secular growth assumptions.

ChangeWave Alliance: A network of open source investing professionals sponsored by *ChangeWave.com* using the ChangeWave Investing model within a broad spectrum of New Economy industrial categories or "spaces." This "distributed-knowledge" community, limited to New Economy knowledge workers, is dedicated to one goal: improved investing results via superior investment intelligence created and delivered every day by ChangeWave Investing system's analysis, logic, and raw intelligence-gathering.

ChangeWave.com: The web site which supports individual ChangeWave investors and ChangeWave Alliance members.

ChangeWave Investing: An aggressive-growth research and analysis model or protocol for New Economy stock analysis and selection.

Dark Zone: The panic attack that investors get during market meltdown periods that drives them to sell their biggest winners to relieve themselves of the "pain" of losing gained profits.

Emerging Game-Over Dominator (E.G.O.D.): The not-yet-dominant leading or co-leading market-share company within an emerged or emerging SuperSector.

FadWaves: A temporary high growth phenomenon caused by the emergence of a mass-market consumer fad. The KVP is a new way to be cool (purchase of the product) with an emotional payoff that (for a while) many people can't resist.

Float: The percentage of a company's stocks that is held by the public and not by insiders. A limited supply of stock means more buyers than sellers for recently public New Economy companies in high demand no-brainer spaces. This supply-and-demand imbalance is what rockets these stocks to their first 500 to 1,000 percent wave of appreciation.

FUD: Fear, uncertainty, and denial—what most people feel when a new technology or industry threatens their existing world.

Game-Over Dominator (G.O.D.): The dominant market-share leader within an emerged SuperSpace.

Gross Profit Margin: The money left after a company pays for the cost of its goods or services sold. We use this screen to eliminate companies that don't have a scalable business. "Scalable" means that the costs to actually produce the service or product of a New Economy company should be relatively fixed so that when unit volume hits critical mass, gross profit margins (sales price minus cost of goods sold) stay high or go higher. A company with a gross margin less than 50 percent does not make it on our team. Seventy percent or higher is our usual cut-off—and many of our WaveRider companies earn 80 percent gross profit margins.

Incremental Change: Synonymous with linear change—change that improves the status quo. Incremental change or transitions are not monster investable opportunities.

Industrial Intelligence Panels (IIPs): Credentialed New Economy members of the ChangeWave Alliance enpaneled within one or more New Economy sector and subsector panels based on their professional expertise, experience, and educational training. The richness and reach of each sector and space IIP members are the main intelligence-gathering tool used to collect and review investable intelligence on emerging ChangeWaves, SuperSectors, and SuperSpaces.

Infrastructure: The enabling hardware, software, and services required in the delivery of a technological solution.

Killer Value Proposition: A new, order-of-magnitude improvement in the status quo or what is known as the "existing value proposition." Massive shifts in customer demand result when entrepreneurs sell and customers adopt new Killer Value Propositions. ChangeQuakes are Killer Value Proposition–enablers—the catalyst for irreversible secular shifts or conversions in customer demand.

MarketStorm: A correction of 10 percent or more of the NASDAQ 100 index (the index which best represents the New Economy) in an overall bull market.

Mission Critical Common-Thread Enablers: This less-than-graceful term describes a uniquely and highly profitable type of SuperSpace and WaveRider company that provides a product or service that is

- Pervasively mission critical throughout many sectors—i.e., a common thread must-have enabling component, application, or service.
- Agnostic—they take no sides in the battles for marketplace domination, so they benefit no matter who wins.

These companies are the ultimate "bullet sellers"—they make money from virtually everyone in the New Economy no matter who wins.

Monster ChangeWave: Shorthand for a macroeconomic or economy-wide secular transition. In the United States economy we consider a secular macroeconomic transition "monsterish" if its revenue is projected to exceed $1 trillion.

Moore's Law: The thesis profferred by the co-founder of Intel, Gordon Moore, that the computing power of semiconductor chips would double every 18 months without additional cost. This increasing return phenomenon is one of the key drivers of high-tech unit growth at lower unit prices.

Moving Average: A average closing price for a stock over a 50-day or 200-day period. The moving average smoothes out day-to-day swings in prices and creates a context in which to judge price trends. Calculated by dividing the number of days (either 50 or 200) into the average price of a stock for the last 50 or 200 days (determined by adding the closing prices for the last 50 or 200 days).

No-Brainer: Something that is so blatantly obvious or easy to grasp virtually everyone gets it.

No-Brainer Disproportionate Reward Rule: The most predictable winner in a top secular growth space goes to the highest market valuation—every time.

No-Brainer Logic Rule: All things being equal, the simplest to understand secular growth and competitive advantage logic wins the growth stock debate.

No-Brainer Predictability Rule: The right stock in the best space gets the money.

Not-at-All Manufacturing: The New Economy business practice of outsourcing built-to-order manufacturing and non-value-adding business processing to more efficient, lower-cost specialist providers. This is the basic formula for the Virtual Corporation Monster ChangeWave: companies focusing on adding value to their services and products with proprietary intellectual property and information, adding shareholder value via proprietary sales and marketing activities, and offloading lower or non-value-adding processes to infrastructure service providers.

Open Source Investing: A cooperative network of securities research whereby industry professionals adopt a common investment research logic and analysis protocol. The network shares their collective observations and peer-reviewed investable intelligence. Improvements to the model are incorporated and updated to all users.

Order-of-Magnitude: A ten times increase in power, magnitude, or benefit of a product or service.

Price Earnings Ratio (P/E): Price divided by earnings per share. Literally means the ratio of a company's stock price to the trailing twelve months' earnings per share. The standard prism by which Old Economy stock pickers attempt to value or "discount" the future earnings of a company. The higher the P/E ratio a company commands, the higher the expectations for future rates of growth.

Pure Play: Refers to the percentage of a company's revenues within a favored industrial space. Typically more than 50 percent qualifies, but 75 percent or more is better.

Secular Change: A long-term sustainable or noncyclical transition or trend.

SpaceMap: A schematic representation of a sector's value chain identifying the enabling spaces within a discrete New Economy sector. It is used to identify discrete spaces and pure play companies within a SuperSector's value chain which stand to most benefit from rapid growth.

SuperSector: An enabling industrial sector directly linked to a Monster ChangeWave that has met our growth threshold of growing at a rate more than 500 percent (5x) faster than the S&P 500 growth rate.

SuperSpace: An enabling industry or market space within a SuperSector that meets our growth threshold of 1,000 percent (10x) faster than the S&P growth rate.

Understructure: The raw components used within the enabling hardware, software, and services required in the delivery of a technological solution.

Value Chain: An enabling subset of components and services spaces that connect ChangeWaves to SuperSectors to SuperSpaces to WaveRider companies to customers.

Virtual Enterprise Genesis: The trillion-dollar shift/conversion from vertically integrated manufacturing and client server–based processing to "Not-at-All" manufacturing and non-value-adding service e-sourcing delivered over Internet Protocol computing architecture from offsite application and infrastructure service providers. As of January 15, 2000, one of the four Monster ChangeWaves.

WaveMap: A schematic representation of the ChangeWave's value chain identifying the enabling beneficiary sectors of the ChangeWave secular growth assumption.

WaveRider: A stock within a favored SuperSpace that best capitalizes on an investment thesis or Big Investment Idea.

Bibliography

Browning, John, and Spencer Reiss. "Think Locally, Act Globally." *New Economy Watch*. February 2000.

Browning, John, and Spencer Reiss. *New Economy Watch*. November, 1999.

Burnham, Bill. *How to Invest in E-Commerce Stocks*. New York: McGraw-Hill, 1999.

Downes, Larry, and Chunka Mui. *Unleashing the Killer App: Digital Strategies for Market Dominance*. Boston: Harvard Business School Press, 1998.

Drucker, Peter F. *Post-Capitalist Society*. New York: Harper-Collins Publishers, 1993.

Du Bois, Peter C. "Chaudhri's Laws—Interview." *Barron's*, May 10, 1999.

Elliott, John. *The Theory of Economic Development*, 4th ed. New Brunswick, Connecticut: Transaction Publishers, 1983.

Evans, Philip, and Thomas S. Wurster. *Blown to Bits: How the New Economics of Information Transforms Strategy*. Boston: Harvard Business School Press, 2000.

Gibson, William. *Neuromancer*. New York: Ace Books, 1994.

Grove, Andrew S. *Only the Paranoid Survive: How to Exploit the Crisis Points That Challenge Every Company*. New York: Doubleday, 1996.

Hamel, Gary, and C.K. Prahalad. *Competing for the Future*. Boston: Harvard Business School Press, 1996.

Hulbert, Mark. "Scary Stuff, Indeed: Halloween as Bellwether." *New York Times*, February 20, 2000.

Hyatt, Joel, Peter Leyden, and Peter Schwartz. *The Long Boom: A Vision for the Coming Age of Prosperity*. Cambridge, Mass.: Perseus Publishing, 1999.

Johnson, Paul, Tom Kippola, and Geoffrey A. Moore. *The Gorilla Game: An Investor's Guide to Picking Winners in High Technology*, 2nd ed. New York: HarperBusiness, 1998.

Kelly, Kevin. *New Rules for the New Economy: 10 Radical Strategies for a Connected World*. New York: Penguin Group, 1998.

Kelly, Kevin. "Wealth Is Overrated." *Wired Magazine*, March 1993.

Laderman, Jeffrey M. "Commentary: We're All Tech Investors Now." *Business Week*, October 25, 1999.

Mandel, Michael. "How Fast Can This Hot Rod Go?" *Business Week*, November 29, 1999.

Mintz, S.L. "The Second Annual Knowledge Capital Scoreboard: A Knowing Glance." *CFO Magazine*, February 2000.

Nakamura, Leonard. "Intangibles: What Put the New in the New Economy." *Business Review*, July/August 1999.

O'Neil, William J. *24 Essential Lessons for Investment Success: Learn the Most Important Investment Techniques from the Founder of Investor's Business Daily*. New York: McGraw-Hill, 2000.

Petzinger, Jr., Tom. "The Front Lines." *Wall Street Journal*, January 1, 2000.

Porter, Michael E. *Competitive Strategy: Techniques for Analyzing Industries and Competitors*. New York: Free Press, 1998.

Raymond, Eric S., and Tim O'Reilly. *The Cathedral & the Bazaar*. Sebastopol, California: O'Reilly & Associates, 1999.

Schumpeter, Joseph A. *The Theory of Economic Development*, 4th ed. New Brunswick, Connecticut: Transaction Publishers, 1996

Shapiro, Carol, and Hal R. Varian. *Information Rules: A Strategic Guide to the Network Economy*. Boston: Harvard Business School Press, 1999.

Tapscott, Don. *Digital Economy: Promise & Peril in the Age of Networked Intelligence*. New York: McGraw-Hill, 1996.

Thurow, Lester C. *Building Wealth: The New Rules for Individuals, Companies, and Nations in a Knowledge-Based Economy*. New York: HarperCollins Publishers, 1999.

Williams, Roy H. *The Wizard of Ads: Turning Words into Magic and Dreamers into Millionaires*. Austin: Bard Press, 1998.

ChangeWave Investing
Track Record

ChangeWave New Economy E.G.O.D. and G.O.D. Stocks
Cumulative Performance (1995–1998 Recommendations)
(Numbers are rounded)

Ticker Symbol	Purchase Name	Purchase Date	Purchase Price	12/31/99 Price	5-Year % Gain
AOL	America Online, Inc.	1/2/95	$2	$83	3,884%
SCH	Charles Schwab Corporation	1/2/96	$8	$37	377%
CSCO	Cisco Systems, Inc.	1/2/97	$11	$108	918%
DELL	Dell Computer Corporation	1/2/97	$2	$51	3,080%
EMC	EMC Corporation	6/1/97	$10	$114	1,040%
EXDS	Exodus Communications, Inc.	10/2/98	$3	$96	3,067%
INTC	Intel Corporation	1/2/97	$14	$87	522%
WCOM	MCI WorldCom, Inc.	3/1/97	$9	$52	485%
MSFT	Microsoft Corporation	1/2/97	$9	$117	1,149%
QCOM	QUALCOMM Incorporated	1/2/95	$3	$179	5,877%
Q	Qwest Communications Int.	11/1/97	$12	$43	258%
RNWK	RealNetworks, Inc.	3/20/98	$10	$116	1,050%
SIRI	Sirius Satellite Radio, Inc.	1/2/97	$5	$41	814%
VRSN	VeriSign, Inc.	4/20/98	$10	$190	1,722%

Average Cumulative Stock Appreciation ('95–'98 recommendations)   1,732%

ChangeWave New Economy E.G.O.D. Stocks
1999 Performance (Numbers are rounded)

Ticker Symbol	Purchase Name	Purchase Date	Purchase Price	12/31/99 Price	1-Year % Gain
AGIL	Agile Software Corp	9/1/99	$47	$215	360%*
ALLR	Allaire Corporation	10/1/99	$57	$151	166%*
AMCC	Applied Micro Circuits Corp	8/26/99	$48	$132	177%*
ARBA	Ariba, Inc.	9/10/99	$70	$192	172%*
ARMHY	ARM Holdings plc	10/15/99	$58	$199	199%*
BEAS	**BEA Systems, Inc.**	**9/15/99**	**$14**	**$70**	**416%***
BFRE	Be Free, Inc.	11/10/99	$26	$70	175%*
BLSW	Bluestone Software, Inc.	10/15/99	$29	$114	296%*
BVSN	BroadVision, Inc.	10/15/99	$54	$189	251%*
CHKP	**Checkpoint Systems**	**8/25/99**	**$79**	**$219**	**177%***
CLS	Celestica Inc.	8/30/99	$22	$53	147%*
CTXS	Citrix Systems, Inc.	10/1/99	$59	$128	116%*
CMGI	CMGI, Inc.	12/31/98	$27	$326	1,126%
CMRC	Commerce One, Inc.	9/15/99	$28	$204	622%*
EXDS	**Exodus Communications, Inc.**	**4/20/99**	**$8**	**$96**	**1,100%***
INSP	InfoSpace.com, Inc.	11/1/99	$56	$213	283%*
ICGE	Internet Capital Group, Inc.	8/15/99	$6	$200	3,233%*
ITWO	i2 Technologies, Inc.	6/9/99	$33	$189	465%*
JDSU	JDS Uniphase Corporation	12/31/98	$17	$188	171%
KANA	Kana Communications, Inc.	11/1/99	$81	$198	144%*
LWIN	Leap Wireless International	12/30/98	$7	$78	1,048%
MSTR	**MicroStrategy Incorporated**	**5/18/99**	**$20**	**$209**	**943%***
MYPT	MyPoints.com, Inc.	12/6/99	$34	$69	104%*
NTAP	**Network Appliance, Inc.**	**8/25/99**	**$32**	**$85**	**164%***
PHCM	Phone.com, Inc.	11/1/99	$110	$121	9%*
PRSF	Portal Software, Inc.	10/15/99	$53	$98	86%*
QCOM	QUALCOMM Incorporated	1/2/99	$6	$179	2,669%*
Q	Qwest communications Int.	1/2/99	$26	$43	69%*
RMBS	Rambus Inc.	5/1/99	$60	$69	15%*
RNWK	**RealNetworks, Inc.**	**1/2/99**	**$18**	**$116**	**548%**
RHAT	Red Hat, Inc.	11/1/99	$89	$232	159%*
SFE	Safeguard Scientifics, Inc.	12/30/98	$26	$190	629%
SSSW	SilverStream Sotfware, Inc.	10/15/99	$32	$111	245%*
SIRI	Sirius Satellite Radio, Inc.	12/31/98	$34	$41	20%
TMWD	**Tumbleweed Communications**	**9/2/99**	**$19**	**$81**	**327%***
USIX	**USinternetworking, Inc.**	**9/15/99**	**$16**	**$65**	**311%***
VIGN	Vignette Corporation	2/27/99	$15	$189	1,157%*
VRSN	**VeriSign, Inc.**	**1/2/99**	**$15**	**$190**	**1,189%**
VRTS	**VERITAS Software Corp.**	**12/31/98**	**$20**	**$142**	**611%**
VERT	VerticalNet, Inc.	4/20/99	$40	$173	332%*
WIND	Wind River Systems, Inc.	8/25/99	$16	$36	132%*
XMSR	XM Satellite Radio Holding	11/23/99	$25	$39	61%*

Average Recommended Stock Appreciation ('99 recommendations)	511%*

*Partial-year purchases are not annualized as is the industry standard. If they were annulized the stock appreciation percentage would be higher.

Boldfaced stocks are mission critical common-thread enablers.

Index

SPECIAL THANKS

As part of the publishing process many people made contributions.

Montgomery Scott Bard, Peter Belowski, Jarratt Bennett, Tom Callahan, Barry Carter, Paul Carton, Tom Connellan, Frank Costenbader, Linda I. Crockett, Michael Drew, Dave Durham, Mike Lauderdale, Alessandra Lippucci, James Lunsford, Nick Moccia, Bill Price, Trent Price, Jennifer Basye Sander, Bob Scarlata, Michael Shulman, Brian Smith, Tim Timmerman, and Ed Williams read the manuscript and provided valuable comments.

Kandi Botello, publications director at Bard Press, supervised the project from beginning to end, working long hours and weekends. Cliff Avery, editor, and Deborah Costenbader, copy editor, each made major contributions. Cliff's years of business editing proved very insightful and improved the quality of the manuscript. Deborah's eagle eye resulted in many critical improvements and her organizational skills helped meet a tough schedule.

A special thanks to you all.

For additional copies of

ChangeWave Investing
$24.95 hardcover

visit your favorite bookstore

or visit our website at
www.ChangeWave.com

or call toll-free
1-800-945-3132

or fax your order to
512-288-5055.

Visa/Mastercard/Discover/American Express accepted.
Quantity discounts are available.

Bard Press

512-329-8373 voice
512-329-6051 fax
www.bardpress.com